"The author has a beautiful style which is easy to understand and to the point. The book has a flow which makes the reading fast and gripping. Taking you into the depth of a women's life, her experiences and her unspoken, unshared challenges. This book talks about infinite wisdom and courage a soul finds to be free. Get your copy today to get a piece of that wisdom and share Tara's life."
- Nisha Singla

"'Nobody tells you this, but sometimes the healing hurts more than the wounds.' We all crave for a book that completely drags you in, makes you fall in love with the characters, and demands that you sit on the edge of your seat for every horrific, nail-biting moment of it! This is one of those books. The book explores some very dark themes that society often turns a blind side to. Despite the fairly innocuous first 20 pages, the title speaks the truth: this is a book of a woman's journey from fear through faith to freedom. With an unapologetically realistic delivery packed with emotion, the author had me thinking long after I was done reading the book. Life lessons, red flags, and the courage to face the unknown. Accepting and forgiving, learning and unlearning all packed into 225 pages of pure percipience. A must read!"
- Tara Dewan

"This book by Vibha is a gut wrenching yet liberating story of a woman's journey that every woman can relate to, having either a sister or a friend or even themselves who would have been through something like this! Women have the power to go though the worst and rise like a phoenix! We have to realise our deep inner strength and this book, Tara, helps you celebrate a woman's strength.
It's a story of not just her and she, it's you and me!"
- Meghna Khanna

TARA

A Woman's Journey
of Faith from Fear to Freedom

Vibha

Castle Mount
Media
2023

CASTLE MOUNT MEDIA GMBH & CO. KG
Burgbergstr. 94c
91054 Erlangen
Germany

Bibliographic information for the German National Library can be found under http://dnb.d-nb.de.

Edited by Anjani Monga
Cover Design by Meilin Siao Bhatt
Book Interior Design by Aryan Enterprises and Meilin Siao Bhatt
Proofreading by Nimeran Sahukar
Distribution Partner in India: Vital Vishwa Publications

ISBN 978-3-948615-26-0 (Paperback)
ISBN 978-3-948615-27-7 (eBook)

*I bring trust from my past to pass on the baton
to the future in trust...*

To

My Parents
Santosh Kumar
Swaran Gurtu

My Sons
Abbhinav
Yash

Note from the Publisher

Dear Readers,

It is with great pleasure and gratitude that we introduce a new author to the international stage: Vibha Gurtu. Her debut book, Tara: A Woman's Journey of Faith from Fear to Freedom, is a captivating tale that will touch your heart and expand your horizons.

Vibha Gurtu brings a unique blend of talents to her writing. Not only is she a gifted storyteller and healer, but she also possesses a profound understanding of human nature through her background in education, sociology and journalism. Her family's prominent position as pioneers in Indian journalism adds an extra layer of authenticity to her work, allowing readers to explore the depths of Indian culture and society.

Tara is a story that transcends cultural and geographical boundaries. Set against the backdrop of India, it follows the journey of a beautiful, young Indian woman as she embarks on a search for truth and freedom. Through the pages of this book, Vibha Gurtu masterfully weaves together the threads of faith, fear, and, ultimately, freedom.

To preserve the authenticity of the story, we have chosen to leave the Hindi words in the text, just as Vibha wrote them. However, for the convenience of our readers, a comprehensive glossary can be found at the end of the book. This glossary will provide a deeper understanding of the Hindi terms and enrich your reading experience.

Tara: A Woman's Journey of Faith from Fear to Freedom is a powerful testament to the resilience of the human spirit and the universal quest for meaning and fulfillment. It is a book that will inspire and provoke contemplation, regardless of your cultural or religious background.

We are thrilled to present this exceptional work to you and believe that Vibha Gurtu's voice will resonate with readers worldwide. We invite you to embark on this transformative journey with Tara and experience the profound impact of her story.

Warmest regards,
Castle Mount Media

Note for my Readers and Acknowledgments

"There is no such thing as darkness; just the absence of Light," said Jess Bowen. I firmly believe in it.

The idea to write this novel came to me when in a one-on-one healing session a newly wedded client shared her story with me. She had not eaten a full meal for months as her mother-in-law tortured her for not bringing dowry in marriage. In my experience of 16 years as a Talk Therapist I have met many people and heard hundreds of stories. I see and hear fear, shame and guilt in the eyes of my clients, in their words and gestures. They approach me for soul healing and in some cases, I work along with psychologists and at times refer to psychiatrists, where needed. The purpose always is to provide the best possible treatment and healing to the client. I try to help them see the reality, to accept their own truth and to identify themselves with their soul's needs. My aim is to give them a purpose to live a fulfilling life in harmony and in alignment with the higher truth, in their present.

Many of these life stories moved and inspired me. I wrote them as stories, blogs or just lessons for myself. In this book, I have tried to thread them into a single string rather than separate narratives. I tied them together with my own spiritual journey and learning. These experiences have been intricately woven into Tara's evolution and how she is able to redefine and recreate her path out of her misery.

Tara is a Sanskrit name. It means a star and symbolises the light of the soul. Tara's story is of an ordinary woman which we all must have heard, read and witnessed around us many a times. Although the characters in the book are fictional, some of you may find parts of yourselves in Tara or probably in other characters. This is merely a coincidence but not surprising as human nature and emotions are finite.

Those who are on the path of higher learning may find themselves stuck in the struggle between the ordinariness that society thrusts upon them and their brilliant, glowing extraordinary self that is aching to be free. The moment we realise ourselves, we become free. It means that we have the liberty to analyse, recognise and accept our own reality. We all are blessed with a sense of knowing. The moment awareness occurs, awakening dawns upon us.

I tell my clients often that a nut remains a nut till it is cracked open. So, whether you are looking for a life purpose or the purpose finds you, it is your free will to make the effort, to take the first step towards the purpose and answer the divine knock. My spiritual experiences are true and real, although I have changed some names and places to maintain confidentiality.

I am deeply thankful to the people who helped me compile and create this work. I thank Anjani Monga who read the raw scripts, edited them and gave a proper form to the story of Tara. Her patience and passion have been extremely commendable. I want to thank Diya Dhar for her time and advice, and Deepika Dahima, a Counselling Psychologist, for putting facts and figures in place.

I thank my friend Chandrakant, who stood by me through this journey of writing the book and empathised with my mood swings. I thank my sons Abbhinav and Yash for being my strongest pillars of support. Last but not the least,

I thank Ramesh, Reshma and Kanti who looked after my house and children, fed me well and let me be myself while I focussed on my writing. The quotes from various people have been credited to them. Quotes with no names are my own learning.

Vibha

Just living is ordinary, Thriving is extraordinary.

"Ouch!" I was hit by a piece of chalk distracting me as I watched birds chirping on the mango tree. The big mangoes hanging down the branches looked juicy and delicious. Maybe, I should climb the tree during recess and get some? I was wondering if they were ripe enough to eat or still a bit raw when I was rudely distracted by the chalk hitting my head. "Tara, can we please pay attention in the class or is there something more interesting outside the window that you would like to share with everyone?" Mrs. Banerjee arched her eyebrows through the spectacles as she glared at me.

I could never inculcate interest in the routine subjects at school. I loved to be in school but not in class. I wanted to learn and gather knowledge but not for the purpose of clearing examinations. I always felt I was a happy child who romanced with the elements of nature, time and space. I could spend hours looking at the parrots around my home, observing how they would enter hollows of trees, unmindful of the world below as they sat perched at the entrance of their home. In a room full of books, time would fly but every minute in a classroom seemed like eternity.

Thankfully, my best friend, Kiran, was always kind enough to do my homework for me while I preferred to escape from the class every now and then. Kiran, the eldest of five siblings, was the responsible one trying to keep me out of trouble. She loved me like a sister, helping me with my studies and feeling happy even if I scored more than her. My group of friends was complete with Kiran and Neel - the social butterfly. He knew all the gossip while I remained blissfully unaware. The three of us shared a strong and selfless bond.

At home, I was the youngest member, with an elder brother, mother and father. Baba, my father, was a learned man and an idealist, who frequently travelled out of town for work. Baba, for me, was my God, with whom I enjoyed a beautiful relationship of honesty and sharing of knowledge. He was a storyteller at heart and through his many anecdotes he introduced my brother and me to a world of different ideologies, thoughts, cultures and lessons. My love for reading books came from him. He had a room full of books ranging from science and religion to history, philosophy and the classics, which he read to us often.

He was a fearless and composed man whose words were well thought through, based on years of experience and wisdom. I learnt to respect the opinions of others from him. No matter what he thought, he would patiently listen to the other person's perspective. He listened to understand and learn, not merely to answer.

My mother was the binding force of the family who held everyone together. She was the soul of the house with her carefully pleated *saree*, red *bindi*, calm persona and a firm voice. Every morning, she would wake up early, get ready, pray to the gods in her little temple and cook food for the family before going to work. She was a passionate teacher and her students loved her.

Maa was my safe space, with whom I could feel free and share everything. She was a super woman and her hugs were the warmest that always brought a smile to my face. During summer vacations or Christmas holidays we loved watching old movies together on Doordarshan and clapped in appreciation for anything we liked. We would make tea or hot chocolate and keep it in a thermos flask to enjoy during the advertisement breaks. I admired Maa who held fort during my father's absence. She never let us feel a void while Baba was travelling. Her emotions were stable and she was in command, respectfully and lovingly.

Bhaiya, my elder brother, was my pride. He simply doted on me. He would get irritated at times for I was clingy, wore his pants and slept holding his hand but he loved me more than anyone else. He taught me how to play cards, chess, carrom board, cycling and kite flying.

My mother often recalled that when I was younger, I would bounce around my brother throughout the house with soft curls flying around my round chubby face. I was a chirpy and inquisitive child who often walked up to strangers and started a conversation. My mother always felt that I was wise beyond my years and yet, child-like.

My growing years were beautiful. I was confident, and felt safe and secure with Bhaiya on one side, and Maa and Baba as rock-solid supports on the other.

Respect is not only a blessing but a choice and a commitment.

As the years went by, I did not realise how the usual humdrum of my house was shaping me subconsciously. Our house was always full of guests and from each guest I learnt new things as I heard the adults talk. Their conversation reflected kindness, thoughtfulness, consideration and an open spirit. My parents welcomed everyone, although now I feel it must have affected them financially but it never showed on their faces. Not once did I see them argue or fight on any trivial matter.

I understand now that it was a progressive household as I never felt the need to hide anything from anyone or to lie as things were accepted as they were. I valued the simplicities of life and nature. In fact, one day when Baba went for his evening walk, he saw me perched on a stool next to the guard's room at the entrance of our colony. He laughed loudly looking at the 47-year-old guard and the 10-year-old me engaged in a deep conversation about plucking mangoes from a tree. At home, Maa recounted how a few days ago our cook was perplexed about how to answer my question, "Why are round *rotis* considered perfect? We should have the freedom to make any shape we like. Would a triangle, square or random-shaped *roti* taste any different from a round one?"

This wonderful environment fostered by my parents was

what I knew. A place where I found love, happiness, hugs and gratitude in abundance. I saw equality and equanimity at home and observed that there were always diverse topics discussed at the dinner table. Everyone was allowed to have their individual opinion. There were debates, dialogues and discussions with no gossip, judgement, belittling, backbiting or lies. Every opinion was listened to and addressed with acceptance.

My brother and I witnessed a peaceful and loving relationship between our parents that was probably projected on us as well. Actually, now as I recall, the only understanding of marriage was what I saw between my parents. Theirs was a bond of trust and respect where each retained their individuality, helped the other grow and evolve, and were proud of one another. Bhaiya and I felt happy when we saw our parents sharing poetry or just sitting together in silence. There was an air of freedom and inclusiveness. At times, I found myself wishing for the same romance and relationship when I would grow up as I witnessed between my parents.

"Maa, I want to be a mother like you," I said to my mother, while twirling her *pallu* around my tiny fingers. "And why so?" she asked, pushing my curls back from my face and kissing my forehead.

"I want to cook, feed, talk and laugh with kids, put on a red *bindi* and drape a *saree* like you," I replied.

The clarity in my voice and the determination in my eyes touched Maa's heart. She put her hand on my head and prayed for strength, courage and happiness for me.

To hear the sound, listen to the silence.

Summer vacations used to be my favourite time as I would go for morning and evening walks with friends and cousins to Lodhi Gardens. I loved being surrounded by family and friends where honest conversations formed the basis of every word. As time flew by, I grew up to be confident and carefree.

This year was different. I had just turned eighteen and was quite excited about it, as anyone would be. My relatives and cousins had left two days ago and while I missed them, I was happy to be alone. For a person who loved to talk, silence offered a strange kind of solace. I would often get lost and transported to another world watching the trees swaying, birds chirping and butterflies kissing the flowers.

That evening, I returned home after a walk with my friends, helped set the table while Bhaiya brought warm dishes from the kitchen. Like any other day, that evening too, dinner was dominated by conversations about interesting information gathered by watching Doordarshan for about an hour. I always read a book before going to bed and I remember going to sleep with a smile on my face that day as the lead detective in the story was very close to uncovering the truth. I was often tempted to read the end first but something told me not to spoil the fun, so I closed the book, put it away and went to sleep.

That night, I was in deep sleep when I heard temple bells ringing loudly. They were so loud that it almost deafened me. It was as if thousands of bells were ringing around me. Startled, I woke up to a blinding light. I had never seen such brilliance before. Just as I was trying to make sense of what was happening, I saw Goddess Durga emerge from the Light.

I wondered what was happening as I had never been an idol worshipper nor was I superstitious. I would watch my mother light a *diya* every morning in her small, beautiful temple in our home. Maa would recite a few prayers before starting her day and encourage us to take blessings whenever we were travelling out of town or beginning any special task.

I did believe in the power of the Light and the existence of a superior being, but maybe not in the stone idol that sat in my mother's temple. For me, praying meant pouring my heart out and having an honest conversation with the Power that resides beyond the known.

I felt an energy I had never felt before. Tears flowed down my cheeks and filled my heart with contentment. The Goddess was bigger than anything I had ever seen. Like the Sun, she radiated immense glow, pulling me inwards with a gravitational force which was unmatched. I could only feel my heart pounding at that moment.

My physical body was dominated by my heart which seemed to be expanding to open out wide and receive the Light. Bells were ringing at a deafening volume as the deity pulled me within herself.

Ma Durga had come alive. I could feel my body breaking into pieces as I merged in with her to become the One before I blanked out.

By the time I returned to my senses, I heard birds chirping and a cool breeze kissing my face.

It was crazy! I lay in bed trying to figure out what had just happened. I felt something had changed within me and yet, nothing had changed visibly. Awestruck, I smiled.

As I lay in bed thinking, the birds continued to chirp as if to soothe me back to sleep and before I knew it, I fell asleep again.

"You are never given a wish without also being given the power to make it true. You may have to work for it however."
- Richard Bach

It seemed unreal for someone who talked so much to have experienced this and still kept quiet. Somehow, I did not feel the need to announce it. What I experienced was beautiful but I felt that it was too personal.

Weeks after this, I had a dream, remembering which my heart fills with sadness even today and a strange kind of understanding, acquired over the years. In my sound sleep, Bhaiya and I were walking along a beach - one of those beautiful picture-perfect spaces that you see in paintings and movies. The sun was setting in the distance, colouring the sky a beautiful shade of yellow, orange and white. Tall palm trees lined up at the edges and soft sand tickled our feet. We walked towards the water and big waves started rolling in. We were enjoying ourselves as we did when we were children. While I was admiring the beauty around me, I suddenly felt Bhaiya's hand slipping from mine.

It felt like holding sand, the tighter I tried to grip it, the faster it slipped away. My heartbeat increased and I started to panic. Bhaiya faded into the ocean and I clenched my fist so tightly that it hurt. The physical pain of my nails digging into my palms was nothing compared to the emotional pain I felt.

I woke up panting and scared. I quickly looked to my side to find Bhaiya sleeping peacefully. Relieved, I drank some water to calm down and went back to bed with an unexplained feeling of sorrow. Over the next few days, I tried to brush the feeling away as a bad dream that had no meaning and got busy with my studies.

Two months later, on an August morning, I had to skip college because of incessant rains. I was splashing the water that had collected in our balcony when the landline rang. I made my way to the phone carefully, to avoid slipping, and picked the receiver on the fourth ring. I froze as the speaker on the other end informed me that my brother had met with an accident.

As he spoke, I remembered the dream in which Bhaiya's hand had slipped away from mine. I felt the same sense of panic that I had in my dream.

The details started coming back to me, vivid and frightening. I quickly called for my parents. A few minutes later, the phone rang again. As I listened, I could no longer feel my brother's hand in mine. It was over. He was gone.

With all my being I wanted this to be a mistake, the news to be untrue and all of this to be a bad dream that I would wake up from and it would soon be forgotten.

I neither wanted advance intimation nor did I want my brother being separated from me. Bhaiya! He used to dote on me. All his toys were mine, his clothes mine, his friends were like brothers to me and under his protection I felt I could conquer the world. He was not only my elder brother but a parent, friend and confidante.

As the news set in, I could not help but think about how my brother's soul must have felt just before leaving his body. A painless pain when the truck hit him. It is said that in sudden accidents, the body dies but the soul gets a shock and hovers around the body for some time. It is difficult for the soul to believe that it has parted from the body that was its home for so long. Bhaiya's soul must have also been in shock.

"I came forth from the Father and have come into the world; again, I am leaving the world and going to the Father." - John 16:28

Death is inevitable. Some die and move on, while others die to live on.

It is said that grieving is important and that is why every culture has its own rules. How we handle loss differs from person to person and community to community. In particular, our response is strongly influenced by our religious backgrounds.

My family had just completed forty days of mourning when one morning, Maa entered my room and saw me lying face down on the bed attempting to muffle my sobs. The moment I felt her hand on my back I burst into a loud cry. Listening to the howling, Baba rushed in.

This was the first time I had hugged them since Bhaiya's death and we grieved our loss together. The three of us cried together and in front of each other. I wanted to hold Maa. I wanted to be close to Baba more than ever. There was no physical injury but something inside of me pained so much that I could not bear it at times. I chose to cut off from life so that I did not have to feel any pain.

Maa kissed my forehead and cheeks, and held my hands in her firm yet gentle grip and said, "Tara, we love you and we understand your loss. Remember that everyone has to die one day. In life, death is the only certainty. Our days are counted, and the time and place of our departure is predestined. It is important to remember that in this life, your brother loved you completely and now he has left for his journey ahead."

As I listened to my mother's words, a part of me wanted to understand the wisdom while the other wanted to reject it. "Untimely deaths are painful and the soul may remain in flux and take time to understand that it has left the body. It is sad and unfortunate but it is the truth," she said.

"I saw Bhaiya's hand slipping from mine. I thought it was a bad dream," I muttered in between sobs. "I saw it," I said. Maa pulled herself back and looked at Baba with an expression I could not understand. Was it fear or understanding? I told them about the dream I had the previous month.

Still holding my hand, Maa sighed and shared that she had been having visions and dreams since she was a child. She too had known about Bhaiya's death prior to the actual mishap. I was shocked to hear this. "I had a vision and I shared it with Baba that the time has arrived for your Bhaiya to move on. There is nothing we can do. In this lifetime, his relationship as our son is complete," she said.

"I wanted to tell him so many things," I told Maa.

"Then tell him. Talk your heart out, tell him everything you want to and then let him go. Do not interfere in his journey of meeting the Light."

I was nervous and perplexed. I asked her to guide me with the conversation.

"Just fold your hands and call upon him as we talk to God.

Visualise him to be here, in front of you and talk to him. Tell him all that you want to," she explained.

I closed my eyes, folded my hands in a *namaste mudra* and called him, "Bhaiya." With tears rolling down my cheeks, I continued, "Bhaiya, where have you gone? I do not know anything. I know only you. You were my guide, my saviour, my best friend. I do not know what I will do without you now. Maa says you have gone forever but I feel you are here and will always be with me. Maa and I had the premonition of you going away. I feel guilty that I could not do anything to save you, Bhaiya. I am sorry. Please forgive me if I hurt you knowingly or unknowingly. Please be around to help and guide me. Maa and Baba say that I should let you go on your onward journey. I free you. I love you, Bhaiya. Please take care of yourself on your onward journey. I love you. Thank you for being my brother, loving me so much and always protecting me." I talked to him till my tears dried up and I was empty. I felt the peace.

I matured overnight.

"The intuitive mind is a sacred gift and the rational mind is a faithful servant. We have created a society that honours the servant and has forgotten the gift." - Albert Einstein

I realised that I had started having visions. My mother's gift had been passed down to me. I could foresee an occurrence about people known and distant, beyond what was visible to the naked eye. It would be a feeling or a vision which appeared. Later, I would get to know that something similar happened with that person.

Maa became my confidante for I did not know who else to share this with. I was still trying to comprehend and understand what had happened.

"Was it not difficult, Maa?" I asked about the premonition.

"There is only so much one can do, the rest is all predestined. Death is a definite reality, the only truth and proof of one's existence. Everything will take place as written. The place, people, surroundings and circumstances are all pre-decided," she shared.

Draped in a white Kota *saree* with a pale-yellow border, she was wearing *sindoor* and a *bindi*. Her long, wet hair was rolled in a *khaadi gamcha* at the nape of her neck. Maa sat in front of her small temple, cleaning pictures and idols of *gurus*, gods and goddesses. I looked at her, admiring her strength, wisdom, poise, dedication and devotion towards her temple, the place of her solace. Maa caught me staring.

Her saintly look focussed on my third eye, the centre between the eyebrows, and closed her eyes slowly signalling me to do the same.

"Always remember, death is inevitable so never be afraid of it or run away from it. It is important to choose how you live rather than be fearful of the end. It is more important to create moments of compassion, forgiveness and joy, and live fully rather than waste oneself by living a fearful and incomplete life," Maa said.

That night, I was reading a novel and was on page seventy-seven of the book where the protagonist, a young woman, was travelling by a train to another city for work. Unable to find a bookmark, I folded the corner of the page and went to sleep. In my dream, I saw myself lying on a railway track, hands tied to the track while a train hurriedly rushed towards me. As I wriggled and tried to free my hands, the train seemed to pick up speed. As it came closer, I saw a figure approach, change the track and the train whizzed past me, inches away from my face. I lay there in disbelief and shock, still tied to the rail.

On the seventh day after the dream, I was travelling by a crowded local bus. Two stops before my destination, I began to feel claustrophobic. Having travelled by buses often, I was surprised at this sudden feeling. Unable to breathe, I got down at the bus stop, untied my *dupatta* and sat at the edge of the pavement trying to calm my breathing, waiting for the next bus.

Suddenly, there was a loud sound and screams all around.

Turning my head around sharply, I saw that the tyre of the bus I had just descended from had burst causing the bus to swerve and hit the pavement and passing vehicles. The dream from last week came flooding back to me. I quickly got up and rushed towards the bus, helping passengers to get off.

I folded my hands and looked up in gratitude.

As months passed, I learnt to be grateful for the time I had spent with my brother. I missed him deeply and remembered him fondly. His demise only reinforced my determination to live life fully. As mortal beings, our time on Earth is fixed. We can either live fully and die gracefully or live in fear of the future, suspicious of the present and regretful of the past.

I made this my *mantra* and thoroughly enjoyed my college years.

During this time, I developed fondness for my classmate, Pritam, who was handsome and outgoing like me. He was quick, smart and fun-loving. There was something in him which attracted me. I could not figure out what it was but we had strong chemistry.

I do not know if it was the idea of romance that excited me or the fact that we were so different from each other. He was hardworking, I was carefree. He was consistent and routine bound, I was consistently inconsistent. He was structured, I was free-flowing. We had different childhoods and upbringing. The dissimilarities and newness intrigued me.

We started dating and within two years decided to tie the knot.

Pritam's mother, Veena, did not approve of me. Before even meeting me, she had expressed her displeasure to Pritam.

When we did meet, she told me within five minutes that she did not want us to get married as she did not like me. Her statement was blunt, honest and quite surprising as I had never met anyone who had expressed such a strong aversion towards me. In my attempt to understand her, I asked Pritam if love marriage was the reason but Pritam told me to ignore her as they did not get along and her opinion did not matter to him. Pritam's father, Dhyanchand or DC, as his friends fondly called him, did not even bother to meet me, the girl his son had chosen but his wife had rejected.

When I introduced Pritam to my parents, they thought him to be a nice young boy. However, when they met his family, Baba, who never spoke poorly about anyone, warned me against them. He had asked around about Pritam's family, as all parents do. He sat me down and advised, "Do not marry into this family. I fear they may never understand you or devalue you. They may cut you short and make a dwarf out of you. Study further and drop the idea of getting entangled with this family."

Baba explained the value of similarity of character of thought between two families in a marriage or any kind of partnership. Similarities strengthen bonds. Similar core values, thought processes, and responses are necessary for a long-term, healthy and respectful relationship. Differences seem attractive initially but have a tendency to fall apart in situations of pressure or as we evolve. Similarities hold everyone together.

Both the families were against this marriage.

It is said one must trust one's gut, heart and head. Gut is

for intuition, heart for emotions and head for logic. All the three were saying 'No' to this marriage and yet, Pritam and I felt strongly for each other.

Eventually, Maa believed that everything was predestined and Baba was confident that one could alter destiny by will, intent and timely action.

Pritam and I decided to get married against all odds and with full trust in our love. Although I listened carefully to my parents' advice, I had read in numerous books and seen in movies that friendship forms the basis of a successful marriage. It is the foundation which builds a relationship and for me the foundation was love. Love could conquer all, I believed.

I thought that in time, everything would be alright. After all, I was marrying Pritam, not his mother. Little did I know then that she would do anything she could to break this bond.

In India, you don't just marry the boy, you marry the family.

While Tara's parents were trying to reason and rationalise with her, Pritam's mother had approached a well-known tantrik to break this relationship.

"I will give anything you ask but please break this match," Veena told the tantrik, a balding man, clad in black clothes, adorning heavy jewellery and sitting cross-legged on the floor. She took out a picture she had of Tara from her purse, disgust visible on her face, and passed it to him. The moment he saw Tara's photograph, he knew she was the blessed one. "Veena ji, why do you want this? The girl seems nice. Why don't you try to convince your son and ask him to end the relationship?" he said, hoping she would not ask him to do what he feared.

"No," Veena replied firmly. "Give me the powder and packets and tell me how to use them. I will do whatever it takes to get what I want." He hesitated, wanting to warn her not from interfering but refrained. He gave in, sensing her determination and his desperate need for money for his own daughter's wedding.

"Veena ji, it would be better if your son calls it off now before they get married and I hope you do not have to use these methods as this girl is a tough one to break. You will have to constantly try to kill her pride, disrespect her and do as I tell you," he said while praying to Goddess Kali for forgiveness. He

then prayed to Goddess Durga and Goddess Kali to protect Tara.

"Now onwards, they will never sleep peacefully," Veena smiled while taking the packets and proceeding to make a list of things she needed to do to pull the young couple apart.

Tara married Pritam against all odds.

FEAR

The soul travels many births and attracts others to learn lessons.

"Thuk, thuk, thuk." I felt as if someone was knocking nails into my soul. First nail, second nail and at the third one, I woke up with a gasp. I saw Pritam running towards the bedroom door. I could still hear the sound ringing in my ears. Confused, I squinted as the lights were turned on and his mother entered swiftly and whisked off the bedsheet to inspect the bed. It was 5:00 A.M.

I stared at his mother who was standing at the foot of the bed with the corner of the bedsheet still in her hand. I looked at Pritam hoping for some explanation. At this point, even if he had shared my surprise, I would have been relieved to have a companion in this puzzled state. Pritam masked his emotions, avoiding my questioning eyes as his mother turned around and left the room.

While I was trying to process this behaviour, I suddenly remembered that I got married to Pritam the previous night. I looked beautiful and felt happy to be with him. Pritam hugged me tight as if he would never let me go. We drifted off to sleep in the midst of making promises of a lifetime to each other. In the morning, the sound of nails being drilled into my soul was actually Veena banging loudly on our door. It scared me a little as I knew my dreams always had a meaning.

That night, I had another vision wherein I was holding Pritam's hand and we were facing multiple challenges. We were strong and could overcome anything. However, every time we dealt with one problem, a new obstacle was thrown our way. After sometime, I felt tired and exhausted. I saw myself sitting on a big, grey rock for a few minutes to regain my strength before starting on a new path.

I could not comprehend much about this vision. On the first day of marriage I hardly had the time or peace of mind to think this through.

On the second day, clothes, jewellery and other gifts were displayed on the *divan* in the drawing room to be shown-off to visitors and relatives who were supposed to come to see the new bride. "I have given my daughter-in-law all these gifts. You see, this jewellery is made in Jaipur and the temple jewellery set is from Chennai. I came to know that Tara loves gold jewellery, so I specially got all of these made for her," my mother-in-law boastfully told her friends.

When the visitors left, she started clearing everything away. Unsure of what to do, I stood there awkwardly. Out of courtesy, I asked if any help was needed. "Back off," she yelled at me. Shocked, I took two steps back. "Do not dare to touch anything. They are for Pritam's wife, the one who will bring dowry, and not for you. You are the daughter of paupers. You never brought anything so why would we give you anything?" she said.

"In fact, do not bother calling me Mummy, Ma or anything of that sort for this relationship will not last long and I would rather die than have you address me as your mother. I would prefer you not calling me at all but if you must, you can address me as Veena," she said and left the room.

I watched her leave. She reminded me of a chameleon. "Why am I thinking this? A chameleon of all things?" It made me wonder.

On the third day she said, "Pritam could get many beautiful girls with lots of dowry. You are not fit to be his wife."

On the fourth day, I was ordered to have a bath with cold water as warm water cost money.

The fifth day, I was denied food because I did not bring dowry.

On the sixth day, I was accused of stealing a silver glass from the kitchen.

On the seventh day, I was given a list of things I was supposed to do and a list of what I dare not. It stated that I had to wake up early in the morning, have a bath with cold water and cook food for everyone, eat after everyone had finished their food, touch my in-laws' feet twice a day, discard all western wear and entertain no visitors without prior permission from my mother-in-law. My parents could not come to visit me nor could I go to see them. Every few days, the list was updated and new dos and don'ts were added to it.

The joy within me was shocked, hurt and abused for taking a stand to marry the boy of my choice and stay firm on the decision to marry without dowry. The first time Veena had mentioned dowry, I actually thought it was a test of my character. I came from a family of high moral values. I never imagined it to be an actual demand. My idealist Baba always maintained that just because the society prescribes something, it does not mean it is right. "Question its genesis and veracity," he said. Maa had taught us the value of education and living with pride. With these ideals forming the foundation of my growing years, I could never have agreed to dowry being given at my marriage.

With every passing day I realised that my ideals and thoughts had no place in this house. As the days went by, I felt as if a game of snakes and ladders had begun for me.

"Let your hopes, not your hurts, shape your future." - Robert H. Schuller

Eventually, Pritam and I shifted to a small one-bedroom apartment with a stove and a bed. We lived like friends, where no one judged the other. Despite financial constraints, we had cultivated a beautiful life. Pritam and I were the couple who spread joy and welcomed everyone. Relatives looked forward to meet us and friends respected and loved us.

Word soon spread about our hospitality. Veena started feeling threatened. She was supposed to be the most sought-after. She had made it clear that she did not like me and yet, relatives were complimenting me. Veena was obviously unhappy with our freedom and growing popularity.

"She is evil," Pritam confided in me one day as he finished a call with Veena.

"No mother can be evil for her own child," I replied, finding it hard to believe that any mother could be such. "She is. I have seen her play games with people. She used to behave very badly with Dadi. She was rude and would ill-treat her but in front of my father she would become the sweetest daughter-in-law. She used to lie all the time. I mentioned this once to my father and since then she has taken me to be her enemy. Be careful of her, she is a devil. I do not want to be like her ever. I hate her."

Honestly, I was shocked by the hatred a son carried in his heart for his mother. Somewhere deep down, I was also relieved that Pritam knew the truth. Pritam and his mother never got along but I had not known until then that it was that bad.

"I always knew that I had to work hard and become something, definitely more than mediocre. For as long as I remember, I have been organised, punctual and ambitious. My teachers always praised these qualities of mine but I did not like it as my mother was also very organised and methodical. She would often scold me that I should be more systematic. I was never good enough for her. Neither was she. She was mean, ignorant and self-centred. She only cared about what the world thought of her. She portrayed the image of an ideal wife, mother and daughter-in-law but at home, she cared for no one. I was all alone until I met you, Tara. I do not want to be like her. Ever. She hates you but you are everything she is not. You would take a bullet for me and be with me no matter what. I know it," he said.

I noticed how he was criticised for his mistakes and according to Veena marrying me was the biggest mistake he ever made. I consoled Pritam, holding his hands in mine, "Everything will be fine, don't worry. We are together now, do whatever you want to. Just be happy." I believed that Veena could do no wrong to me or us, now.

Time passed by and with each month we added something new to the house. I loved to decorate the small, cosy flat with string lights and small pots with herbs out in the balcony. I remember how excited we were when a small green capsicum appeared in one pot and two baby tomatoes in another. I used to plant seeds and would wait eagerly for the flowers to bloom.

On the other side of life, every time we returned from visiting his parents, he would be silent for days and I would cry unendingly.

He promised he would stand up for me, protect me and keep me away from his mother yet we visited his parents every month.

Once a boy matures at thirteen, he should be given freedom to experience his rights. Once he is married, parents should stop controlling him as his duties of a husband begin. The newly married should be left alone to evolve and learn as a couple and understand each other's wants and needs.

Is it because of the patriarchal and patrilineal social system in India that often a son is kept under the thumb of the mother and made to feel guilty if he is happy with his wife? It is commonly heard that the life of a daughter-in-law is controlled and expectations from her are higher than from a son-in-law.

Many believe that a woman needs a man for her security and protection. As a result of this, she is under the protection of her father and brother before marriage and afterwards, the husband and son. Additionally, since women were kept financially dependent, they learnt skills to manipulate either by hook or by crook and always be in command to control the men and household politics. The men made women financially dependent and the women made them emotionally dependent. A scene I was seeing in my new family.

Betrayal never comes from your enemies.

The 'honeymoon period' went on for almost a year. No matter what happened, we always found our way back to each other. However, few months into the second year he took me to my parents' house and left me there for six months. When he dropped me off, all seemed okay and yet, he left without mentioning when he would come back. I longed for him and waited as months passed by. I wrote letters and tried calling him but it seemed he had vanished. When he returned, he pretended like nothing happened.

Another time, a friend called to inform me that Pritam was spotted at a social gathering with an unknown girl. He told everyone there that I was unwell whereas I was perfectly fine and he had not even informed me about the event. To make matters worse, he jokingly introduced the girl to my friend as his new girlfriend.

Few months after that, I had become friends with a neighbour's daughter and we would have a great time together. Suddenly, she stopped coming over and within a week it was heard that the family was shifting to a new residential society. On enquiring, I came to know that the girl and Pritam had an affair and the family found out about it and decided to move.

Every time such incidents happened, Pritam had some

reasoning to justify the action and I found excuses to forgive and forget. "There are no problems between us. It is all in your head. You are overthinking," he would say.

I now feel that as we were very young when we got married. We did not know much about marriage except being in love and together through the thick and thin of it. I also understand now that we came from different thought genres. I did not see the differences and neither did he. Probably it was an infatuation which outgrew itself slowly and we were running out of common desires or maybe the world offered more interesting factors to distract and gave opportunities to digress from the common goal of marriage, love and respect.

It had been three years since our marriage. In these years, we had seen a stable job, the pink slip, moments of distress, finding another job and eventually, Pritam and I challenged the odds and started our own company. While we were finding our footing with the business and improving financially, his parents were a continuous source of concern and bickering. I remember how the most trivial issues were noticed in family get-togethers which were followed by a string of complaints. At first, we used to share our hurts and console each other, trying to overlook the darker side and just feel blessed to be together.

I feel in hindsight that Veena's constant fault-finding was beginning to influence Pritam. How else could I find an excuse for Pritam's behaviour this time. Not only had his temper got out of hand but he had started lying to me and cheating as well. I could never have imagined Pritam doing this. My Pritam? No!

I could not stop crying as I lay on the bed, wanting to die. I kept touching my growing belly thinking of my baby, who was unaware of the reality of the house into which he or she would soon be born. I knew something was fishy between Pritam and his new business associate. It had been almost three months and they had been spending too much time with each other. That day she confessed to me about their affair. "I do not think he loves you. If he did, he would not be with me every evening while you are pregnant. No husband would want to miss these beautiful days," she said.

As I lay in bed, my mind wandered to the past and I connected the dots. Everything that was happening was not a one-off incident. Few months earlier, I had called a beautician who shared having visited my home in my absence wherein there were two more men in the house. When I confronted Pritam, he casually dismissed it saying it was for his friends. I was shocked that Pritam had opened our house for such meet-ups in my absence.

I confronted Pritam about his affair with the associate. He got defensive, abusive, threw a vase at the TV and left the house. When he returned after four days, he asked for forgiveness. Pritam was aloof. The way he spoke and behaved was not his usual self. We maintained the façade and life continued but this time a difference was felt.

I was losing confidence in our relationship, started doubting myself and began questioning my existence for nobody had ever behaved so rudely and rashly with me other than Pritam and his mother.

"If you are going through hell, keep going."
- Winston Churchill

A perfectly beautiful baby. I still remember my baby's face as I sat admiring my four-month-old. I could just look at the little bundle of joy all day. Even though it was amazing, I have to be honest, it was exhausting! Yes, becoming a mother is a wonderful feeling but makes one paranoid too. Every sneeze used to make me wonder if I should call a doctor. The initial months flew by quicker than expected.

As the baby was growing, I was getting back to my earlier life again - meeting friends, having people over and spending time with family. Pritam had two more affairs in the meantime, we had fights, things got ugly, he apologised after a few days and we reconciled.

Time passed and every now and then, I wondered if I was on the right track. If this would be our last fight. If this would be the last time Pritam threw something or misbehaved. Every time he left the house after a confrontation, I wondered why we were still staying in the marriage. Was it because we had hope? Was I in this marriage out of love, habit, child, money or society? It is our desire to have a good reputation in society but the harsh reality is that divorced women are often labelled as troublemakers, feminists, threats, rebels and the list goes on. The biggest problem is often economic insecurity. I had helped Pritam start a company. What would I do, if not this?

Maybe, it was the fear of the unknown. It is said that a known devil is better than an unknown one. Leaving Pritam could be easier than living with him but what about our little baby? We both loved our child. Even though mindsets were changing, still I felt children learn from what they see. In disturbed marriages, they see anger, frustration, bickering, neglect and sometimes develop an aversion to marriage or assume this behaviour to be normal.

Was my parents' marriage an exception?

No matter what the problem was, I loved Pritam deeply and wanted to try to resolve these issues as soon as possible. I knew he did too. Or at least I wanted to believe it to be the reason he sought forgiveness for his actions. I believed that loved ones deserved forgiveness and every person be granted a chance to retrace their actions and be able to make course corrections. I hoped my love and forgiveness were reason enough for Pritam to mend his ways. He had said he would not misbehave again. He had promised.

Every morning, I said my prayers to Lord Shiva, followed by meditation, for it offered me solace and insight, but I was none the wiser regarding my marriage. A situation seemed better when there was silence after a storm. Alas, this lasted only until the next turbulence arrived.

To err is human,
To forgive is being humane,
To ask for forgiveness is courage,
To retain the trust is integrity.

Two years passed by and amidst all the fights and reconciliations, I missed my periods and the home test kit displayed two coloured lines. I was pregnant again. When we shared the news, Veena told me to abort the child.

Veena and DC were disappointed when they found out that Tara and Pritam had reunited. She felt betrayed as it seemed that all was well between the couple. Why else would they have another child? Little did she know that the packets she had hidden in their house were still there, casting an evil spell.

"Do not worry. I will separate them one day. Trust me," Veena promised her husband.

You cannot miss a sign from the Universe. It will keep getting louder and louder until you notice it.

As the company expanded, we worked as equal partners. Pritam was the administration expert and I was the people's person. The business had its own highs and lows but our hard work was starting to show results. We were busy day and night and along with work, I managed the house and the baby.

Creating a balance between work and home is taught to girls more than to boys in India. We observe our mothers and aunts doing it and our daughters see us. At times, I would speculate and share this with my friends about how it is taken for granted that a woman takes all the responsibilities and is expected to do it well too.

During this time of maintaining and retaining the balance I was introduced to Reiki. I had begun with meditation and within months was initiated to different healing modalities.

From here on, I noticed how my life had started running on two parallel tracks. On one side was the house where Pritam, our children and his parents were. We had a 'picture-perfect family' that was fragmenting from within. There were moments of love, forever shadowed by chaos, anger, distress and resentment. On the other side, was my spiritual journey. As I embarked on this road, my visions started coming back, the gift my mother had passed on to me that seemed have been lost during these trying times at home. They were infrequent but they were there lying dormant deep within me.

As you read my story further, you will observe that spirituality grounded and rooted me, took me higher and became my saviour every time I lost hope and moved away from my path. It re-centred me each time I went haywire.

It showed me ways through omens and also created new paths for me. I only had to wake up, get up and take the first step. The rest was taken care of by the Universal Powers.

To know is good,
To know the unknown is blissful.

With the second baby, I expected it to be easier this time but I soon realised how wrong I was. I was busier than usual. During meditation, I focused on my womb. Just as I began, a tall, bald *Sanyasi* with a *kamandal* and stick appeared in front of me. He was leading a group of followers, all dressed in saffron.

He stopped, looked straight into my eyes and said, "Join me in this journey." Surprised at the direct invite and unsure of what to say, I folded my hands and replied, "I have small children. How can I?" I felt sad but knew in my heart that this was the correct response.

He sat down on my left side, put his *kamandal* down and crossed one leg over the other at ninety degrees. Resting his hand on the stick, he started chanting *mantras* I had never heard of before. I folded my hands in a *namaste mudra* and closed my eyes.

It seemed like a few moments but to my surprise the clock showed that thirty minutes had passed when the chanting stopped. As I opened my eyes, he blessed me, lowered his right leg, picked up his *kamandal* and got up. As he walked away, I heard my baby cry and quickly leapt up. Soon, I got busy and almost forgot about this incident.

After two months, I met a *Svetambara*, a Jain *muni*, in a Jain *mandir*, where I had gone with my childhood friend, Kiran. He was clad in white. As soon as we met, he looked at me and said, "I believe you are pregnant. God bless you." Surprised, I told him that I have a small baby at home but I am not pregnant.

Confused, he shared, "The soul of a saint was meant to come into your womb for the last birth (*moksha*) before merging into the Light." As soon as he said that, I had goosebumps as I suddenly remembered the *Sanyasi* who had visited me and recounted the story.

The *muni* listened to me intently, understanding what had happened and explained to me that the *Sanyasi* would have come to my womb to complete his remaining journey on Earth before attaining *moksha*. Since I told him that I would not be able to join him on his journey, he prayed for me and my children, and left. He also shared that the *Sanyasi* had only few years left to fulfil on Earth and if I would have carried him, the child would have passed away young.

As I stood in front of the mirror and draped my peach silk *saree*, I was almost ready to go for dinner to a friend's house. Pritam took out his waistcoat from the closet, stood a few steps behind me and said, "I like Ritika and she likes me. There is no need to make a scene. Just accept it and move on."

My hand stopped midway while applying the cherry-pink lipstick. I looked at him in the mirror, our eyes met and he shrugged his shoulders. Ritika was his friend's wife.

An argument occurred, he threw his waistcoat on the bed and walked out of the room banging the door loudly. I usually picked up the stuff he threw in anger but that day, I let it be. I finished applying my lipstick, shaped the curves properly with the lip pencil, tucked away a stray hair and gave myself a final look in the mirror for my approval before leaving.

I picked up the gift from the dining table and told the driver to start the car. On the second intersection, the driver informed me, "Sir is behind us."

Dear Diary,

It has become so common for Pritam to lie to me that I do not know when he is telling the truth. Is he manipulating me? It seems as if I am dealing with two Veenas. This behaviour and such tactics are what his mother would resort to.

I am confused with this changing behaviour of Pritam which is starting to form a pattern. Oh God! Please show me the way and please take care of Pritam and my family. I do not want to hurt or be hurt but I do not know what to do.

- Confused
Tara

My pen stopped as I wiped my tears and closed the diary. I hid it in my closet, between the clothes, scared in case Pritam found it.

Losing love, respect, intimacy and understanding starts decaying a relationship.

To be in control is one thing and to have the desire to control everything is another. You stop enjoying and are controlled by your greed to be powerful by acquiring external possessions. There is always a void and it is a mirage to feel that possessing material things makes one happy. This could be observed when Pritam bought the top model of cars launched in a given year, sold it the next year and then bought another top model the following year.

Interestingly, we have a fifty percent chance to become what we hate the most as both the extremes are present in the same pole. We make our choices and excuses, and both have the opportunity to flourish.

I started socialising with women from diverse professional backgrounds and during a meet-up, one of them shared about a handsome, rich man who had asked her out but she was hesitant as he was also her business client.

Everyone gushed and asked to see his photograph. The mobile was unlocked, the picture searched and the phone placed on the table for everyone to see. "Handsome indeed," I said and smiled as I recalled clicking this picture of Pritam lounging on the beach. It was from our vacation in Sri Lanka.

So this is the picture he is using these days.

I immediately cut the thoughts with the NO response theory and stopped myself from thinking on those lines. I feared my thoughts would go astray if not checked. It is the thought we feed that germinates. When you think of something once, it grows, but if you give it constant attention, it thrives.

These meetings with the ladies had taught me many things:

- ❖ Women are strong
- ❖ Women are emotional
- ❖ Insecure parents bring up insecure children
- ❖ Earning money gives women strength and the freedom to spend gives them courage and confidence
- ❖ It is a belief carried forward that women need marriage to feel secure
- ❖ Women can be manipulative
- ❖ Women have secrets
- ❖ Women are strong yet insecure
- ❖ Women doubt themselves

I was cautious yet free with these women. I did not have to reveal much about myself while they served as a good distraction. I could enjoy myself with them without Pritam objecting and I heard stories of many kinds, silently.

I preferred to ignore some and learn from the rest. The talks were educating me and also questioning me about who I was and what I wanted to be.

Attachment encages you and love liberates you.
In the former, you want the person to be available for you,
Latter allows you to be yourself.

It seemed as though Pritam and I were stuck in a vicious cycle. One of us would do something that would result in a fight. We would argue and then Pritam would either get angry, bursting into a rage and throwing things around or give me silent treatment and go away somewhere. This would often be followed by him gifting me something expensive to make up. I had a Rado watch, a mark near my ankle from when the glass shard from the vase he threw pierced me, a diamond ring, a burn mark from the hot *dal* on my left arm when he banged the table in a fit and a lovely holiday in Dubai. Things would get better only to become worse.

The perfect house had the self-made entrepreneur, a beautiful wife and well-mannered children. Each year, a new car or property was added to the list. Inside the perfect house, our conversations were diminishing and I was starting to get scared of Pritam, and his unpredictable moods and behaviour.

My mother, a wise woman, had given me three choices to live:

❖   Move out of this abusive marriage

- ❖ Create boundaries
- ❖ Get busy with studies and kids

I began to visit a counsellor and in one of the sessions, I confessed that our marriage had begun to erode and I did not know what to do to save it. The image of love and marriage with Pritam that I held close to my heart was losing its shine. I was confused whether his affairs came between us or the affairs happened because we were growing apart. Both cases could be true yet, Veena's hatred was the only consistent factor in every variation. She continued to berate me at every opportunity she got, trying to convince Pritam that he had made a mistake by marrying me and that he should rectify it before it became too late.

Even though I was losing interest in wanting to look good or make an effort to dress up, I kept myself smart and in shape. I learnt how to apply make-up the right way and had mastered the technique to cover my sadness and loneliness. "Make-up is done to camouflage flaws and enhance the beauty," the trainer had shared.

I told Farida, my counsellor, that my sole desire was to feel loved. I cried like a baby as I acknowledged what I wanted and admitted that I hated what I was becoming, a weak and broken woman.

My freedom was controlled starting from where I went to whom I befriended. At heart, I yearned for a friend who was not pre-approved by Pritam. He made sure that I was friends with only those he agreed of. In need of an outlet, I volunteered at NGOs, joined many new courses, looked after the kids' hobbies, hosted dinners at home and made friends with books.

I tried to make myself happy with my children, spending time with other mothers in salons and having lunches with my friends but the façade did not last for long. In reality, I was living a life of a 'housed wife' within the four-walls.

My hobby of reading books became my escape route and brought me closer to introspection amidst the many self-help, spiritual and meta-physical books. I realised that in every religion, silence was encouraged to calm the mind, replace reactions with responses, discover inner strength, find oneself, get connected to the higher self and understand that along with all this, awareness was the ultimate goal for all.

Blessings come in many forms. Be open to receive in gratitude.

One morning I received a call from a dear friend who had invited a well-known priest from one of the most revered temples in India. Even though I did not like being in crowded areas or events and often excused myself from attending such social gatherings, this time I felt a pull to accept the invite. At heart, a small group of family and good friends is what gave me true joy. I enjoyed meeting new people but often found large social gatherings exhausting and overrated.

As I entered the large foyer, I heard the priest speaking. I chose a quiet corner from where I could hear the verses and their explanations and still be away from the crowd. There was sound as well as silence, the sound of the verses as the priest recited and silence among the devotees.

Some sat with folded hands, while others stood on the sides but everyone was glued to the mesmerising voice and the persona of the priest. As the verses ended, loud praises were chanted in the name of the Almighty. Everyone stood up with folded hands and made way for the priest to take leave and retire for the day.

Dressed in a white *kurta* and *dhoti* with a saffron border, he held a *mala* in his right hand. I closed my eyes and folded my hands in a gesture of respect as the priest was nearing. Blessing everyone he passed, he stopped in front of me and asked my name. Surprised, I opened my eyes, looked up and answered, "Tara".

He smiled and said, *"Darti kyun ho? Jaano tum kaun ho. Shakti ho! Sone ki tarah mazboot bano aur chamko. Daro nahi.* Ma Durga *tumhare saath hai, tum surakshit ho."* (Why do you fear? Know who you are. You are strength! Be strong like gold and shine. Do not be scared. Goddess Durga is with you. You are protected)

With that he recited a *mantra* and put out his hand as if to offer me something. I received the blessing with open hands and thanked him. As soon as I reached my car, I opened my fist. I was in awe when I saw a beautiful gold locket of Lord Ganesha.

Marriage is a gamble. Know the rules well.

Pritam's friend came for dinner and shared news about his newfound love. The twinkle in his eyes, excitement in his voice and the constant smile was a refreshing sight. He kept talking about the girl, her personality, features and his love for her. I started visualising the love and romance while listening to him. I could actually feel the warmth of their togetherness when Pritam's voice interrupted my thoughts.

He talked about the time when he first saw me and how his heart had skipped a beat. How he used to love me and stand in a queue for almost an hour at the telephone booth to talk to me. "You are not the only romantic fool. I used to be totally gaga over her," he said, mocking his friend.

The friend laughed and pointed out that all of Pritam's sentences were in the past tense. "Where is the love now, brother?" he asked.

The chat was a trigger.

Pritam brushed aside the question and invited him for a stroll. As they both left, I only thought of the conversation as I put away the dishes and changed my clothes before retiring to bed.

He might flirt with women, spend money on them and cheat on me but he always came back home and took his place at the dinner table. No matter how deep the rift was between us, he would always thank me and everyone for the food at the end of dinner. I took it as a coded apology for his infidelities and I forgave him. I always did.

The difference between eye and eyehole is that one sees and the other allows one to see through.

"Ouch!" I yelled as Pritam grabbed my wrist, pulled me up from the chair and pushed me out of his cabin. The love of my life stripped off my pride, crushed my self-belief and smashed my self-respect.

He had called me to his office that day and the moment I sat down opposite him, he started a monologue that went on and on. He said my performance was not up to the mark in the office, I was failing him, and was a let down, a disgrace to his reputation and a disappointment overall. His voice changed and eyes became red, just like his mother's when she got angry.

It was the first time he shouted and screamed at me in the office while the staff was outside. The cacophony deafened me. I sat still, unable to move as he kept humiliating and disrespecting me. His words echoed Veena's, "You are useless and good-for-nothing. I could get a better girl. It was a mistake to have married you." I could almost hear her voice as he finished his sentence using the same words. Every word felt like a stab as I sat opposite him in his office. I could feel myself going blank.

He rose from his big, brown chair, walked across the table and stood next to my chair, turned me around to face him and squeezed my shoulders tightly till tears rolled down my cheeks and said, "You are an ugly woman. You have nothing to give me anymore. Mend your ways or else…"

He grabbed my wrist, pulled me up from the chair and pushed me out of his cabin. Veena had pushed me out of her house twice.

As I drove back home, I could still feel the pain in my wrist, the scene replaying in my head, the harsh taunts echoing in my ears. I reached home and ran to my room.

That day something broke inside me. I was dead and yet living. I knew it was because I had peeked through that keyhole two days ago. I just knew it. It was confirmed when the person in-charge of security cameras nervously told me in confidence that the office camera recording was sent to Pritam every day. I thanked him for having the courage to tell me the truth. Somehow, I knew that Pritam would fire him for this. I hoped that he would never find out but unfortunately, the employee simply stopped coming to work without anyone's knowledge.

Two days ago…

With a small baby at home, I had stopped going to the office regularly and managed urgent matters from home. Soon, I learnt that the newly appointed Radhika, who was supposed to assist me had suddenly been shifted to Pritam's team and later became his secretary.

I did not find anything amiss until I joined office full-time within two weeks of hiring her. It was then that I noticed the closeness between the two. There were rumours about them as Pritam would eat lunch with Radhika every day, have long closed-door meetings with her much too often and drop her home every evening. Interviewed and hired by me, the once respectful Radhika evaded me now.

One evening, as I was half-way home I realised that I had left my laptop in the office and returned to get it as there was an urgent email to be sent. As soon as I crossed Pritam's cabin, I heard a strange sound from within followed by a giggle. The office was almost empty. Surprised, I looked through the keyhole. Two shadows were standing uncomfortably close to each other. I recognised them and instantly pulled myself back. I felt nauseous. I could not see anymore nor did I want to. I immediately tried to erase the image from my conscious mind. It was too embarrassing for me to even acknowledge what I saw, let alone share it with anyone else.

It was quite funny that till the time I had not seen the act, it was easier for me to ignore the facts. Yes, he was having an affair. So, what? That was not new but that day reality hit me hard. I realised that it had been more than three months since we actually had sex. The intimacy which Pritam and I shared had vanished between the hurts, abuses, kids, office and parties. The façade was getting bigger and the veil thicker. A lot had been brushed under the carpet. I became motionless and silent.

Silence and I shared an old camaraderie. In silence, I could find my centre. In silence, I could listen to my heartbeat and quieten my mind.

This time, I felt numb.

I mustered up the strength to pick up my laptop and rush to the car. I followed the green light *mantra* which I had developed along the years. It might have been the longest route to return home but whenever something bothered me deeply, I drove non-stop, the only goal being to declutter my thoughts and get clarity. As the vehicle moved without stopping, so did my mind, freeing all obstacles and blockages. It is a *mantra* I swear by and that day I needed it the most.

If you are alive, your purpose is still incomplete.

What is the point of living a life without love, respect and hope?

I wanted to live a simple, graceful and respectful life but the more I tried, the harder it got. The more I forgave, the worse it became.

Somehow, I could not understand why the need to live and the desire to lead a fulfilling life was slipping from my hands. I did not know what to do. I did not know why I was living. Was it because of my children or because I did not want to hurt my parents as they had already lost their son?

It was one of the darkest days of my life. I gave up on myself. I came back home wanting to end this. I had no will to live. Unable to control myself, I kept crying and asking for forgiveness and help from Shiva, my saviour.

I did not realise when I dozed off to sleep on the wet pillow. In the state of deep sleep, I felt my soul leaving my body. I felt dead. There was nothing left in me. I felt light and heavy at the same time. Heavy as if the body was lying dead and weightless as if the soul had left the body.

Suddenly, I was surrounded by light and I saw the faces of everyone I loved and behind them stood Shiva. Bhaiya was the first one to step forward and I ran to him crying, "Take me with you. I no longer want to be here. Please."

He gently wiped my tears and said, "I love you, Tara. This is a self-defeating thought. Kill this thought not yourself. You may have lost a lot, but I know you have not lost yourself. This is not the kind of ending a gifted soul and an empowered person like you can have. You have your Shiva by your side. What else do you need? Trust in yourself like you do in Him. Remember, I am always by your side to protect you."

I looked at the deity behind him, the serene eyes seemed to read my mind. I started walking towards him and with every step my surroundings disappeared.

This was the second time I felt suicidal but that day, I woke up feeling as if the thought had left me forever.

It felt strange and beyond my understanding. I knew it was an unknown power but it made me wonder why I considered suicide. To end this suffering of course, my subconscious mind almost rolled its eyes at my silly question.

It was too much to endure the hurts and abuses but I had forgotten that I was strong enough to stand up and put an end to it.

If I did take my life, people would gossip, friends who loved me would be angry and sad for some time, my children would be shocked and scarred for the rest of their lives, and my parents would die before their time.

The circus of inquiries and allegations would start. Eventually, everyone would get busy, friends would find new friends and my spouse would get a substitute. I would be replaced and forgotten till the next news of a suicide.

I realised that my Shiva had helped me. He had pulled me out of this dark hole which I may be unable to describe properly for it was the worst sort of hell. One can only imagine how bad it was for me to have wanted to end my life. Yet, I often worry about those who do not have a saviour helping them.

I came out of it because the thought which was hovering strongly in my head was replaced by reason and a goal. I decided to fight it till the end. "It is better to die fighting rather than shoot oneself before the war," Baba always said. I never thought his words would have such a literal meaning in my life.

There is nothing like a vacuum. Everything, almost everything, is replaced and restored in a different name, shape and form. There is only the presence in its absence which is created, recreated and realised till the ultimate is arrived in soul levels and reached on physical planes.

FAITH

If life is a gift, then living a half-life is worthless.

Have you ever noticed how an infant behaves when brought to a new place? First, they observe the surroundings from the safety of their loved one's arms. They are inquisitive yet cautious. Then slowly, as they feel a little more comfortable, they crawl around wanting to explore the space but remain in the vicinity. It is only after this that they are confident enough to venture alone.

Similarly, I was earlier being cautious with the visions and thoughts. A little wary yet, grateful. As I progressed with my meditation, I gained confidence and started getting experimental. I was still crawling in a safe space not trying to be overly adventurous. I was making and creating my own ways to reach the Light for a composed, calm and peaceful self.

Wanting desperately to escape the turmoil of the house, I visited a friend who was posted in Yol, Himachal Pradesh, which was an hour's drive from McLeodganj, home to His Holiness, the Dalai Lama. I had wished to meet him and mentioned this to my friend, who was quick to respond that His Highness (HH) was busy with his meditation and would only be able to meet visitors on certain dates, subject to last minute changes. I told my friend, "Let me also sit in meditation and send him an aerial message."

The next morning, I sat for my meditation and as I was inching and exploring the new area whilst in my safe space, I attempted to send a message to HH, the Dalai Lama. The request was sent and to my surprise, I received a message on my birthday that the appointment had been fixed. I could not believe it!

Often, when we are at our lowest, a glimmer of hope comes in different ways and forms. For me, it was this meeting.

I reached McLeodganj. I still remember the first glimpse of His Holiness. As I stepped in front of him, mesmerised by his aura, I felt calm, peaceful and grateful to be in his presence. With folded hands, I asked earnestly, "Should I cease to exist?" He smiled a little, touched his forehead to mine, held my face in his hands and said softly, "See…wait to see what life offers you."

I could see the beaded *mala* on his left wrist before closing my eyes to receive his blessing. It was as if he had infused new life into me.

At that moment, I felt that in my quest for a ray of hope, I received the entire rainbow. Within seven days of meeting His Holiness, I got an invite to travel out of the country to attend a course. It was the first time I was travelling alone internationally. Being alone did not necessarily mean being lonely. It was often a chance to be independent, free and being with oneself confidently.

Over the years I had almost forgotten who I was and the trip healed me in many ways. New learning always excited me. With the new learning and new people, I had a wonderful time. Even amongst strangers there, I could be myself and everyone respected me and my thoughts. I loved the honest and unbiased conversations.

Tara - a star, a source of light, the one Goddess Durga had blessed. I realised I had become hunched under the pressures and abuse.

We often forget who we are and sometimes, choose to forget because of a few instances of judgement or criticism. On the surface, I seemed happy, confident and carefree but felt the exact opposite inside. In this new land, I felt accepted for who I was. I could see admiration and acceptance in the eyes of those strangers. My words were listened to without judgement. It was like taking baby steps to share my ideas freely without the fear of being rejected, ridiculed or disliked.

I felt alive and liberated!

Universal secrets are revealed in many forms. The deal is to open your senses.

As Pritam scouted a new car he wanted to buy, the four of us went to a well-known showroom for high-end cars. The children looked around with their father and I sat on a fluffy, white couch, casually scrolling through my phone, waiting for them to decide which car they preferred. After twenty minutes, I was shown a pre-owned car that looked almost brand new and was told that the specifications were great.

As I was being told about the car, I scanned its energy. Suddenly, I saw fire in my vision and people getting out of the car and dusting their shoulders, as if to shake off ash. On sharing this with the people at the showroom, they dismissed it. They were asked again about the history of the car and if such an incident had occurred, but they declined, a little displeased at being asked again. They offered to email the car's records for our satisfaction.

Trusting their word, the car was brought home with a promise that within a day the records would be sent to clarify matters. However, three days passed and no records were sent. Miffed at this, Pritam emailed the parent company of the car brand which had its headquarters abroad. They responded that the details would take twelve hours to be shared.

True to their word, we received the information in twelve hours, and within ten minutes, the car keys were picked up and Pritam drove to the showroom. He showed the email and returned the car. He felt cheated and angry while the people at the showroom were shocked at being caught and took the car back, embarrassed. The records said exactly what I had seen in the vision that the car had met with an accident and caught fire. However, the occupants had been safe and no one was hurt.

Sitting cross-legged on the floor one afternoon, I leaned over the family albums looking for pictures for my younger one's school project. It opened a Pandora's box. Happiness, romance, love, bonding and fun times dominated our faces. As I opened another album, I saw pictures from when Pritam and I were in college together. Young love was visible on our faces and smiles conveyed the romance we shared.

"Pritam and I were inseparable then," I thought, "and now we hardly even slept in the same room. Friends used to call our names together even if only one of us was present. We used to laugh and bring joy wherever we went. We would brighten up the place with our happy and high energy." As I turned over the pages, I came across a picture with his parents and then my parents. What a stark difference! Our smiles had vanished in the picture with Veena and DC. There was suffocation visible on our faces as we posed.

Later that day, I got busy preparing dishes Pritam had desired to be made for dinner as he had invited his friends.

Drinks were served, snacks were rolling in and voices got louder with each drink.

"Marriage is crazy. At first love keeps you going and after a few years, you have to keep it going as love flies out of the window," joked one of his friends.

The other quoted Kahlil Gibran, "Every man loves two women, one is the creation of imagination and the other is not yet born."

The men continued to crack such jokes as I served some snacks to each, quietly listening to them. Their laughter only increased as they raised their glasses to cheer and recite, "Every man loves two women."

"Every man loves two women, one mother and one daughter."

"Every man loves two women, one wife, one daughter."

"Every man loves two women, one at home and one in the office."

"Every man loves two women, one whom he loved and one whom he loves."

"Every woman loves two men, one known and one unknown". There was pin drop silence as I said this.

Uncomfortable glances shot across the room till one of them, a little too tipsy, laughed loudly and said, "Every woman loves two men, her two dogs."

"Every woman loves two men, one from the head and one from the heart," said another.

Quite wise, I thought at the last one and the jokes continued.

Later that night, I was fast asleep when Pritam entered the room after his little party. He switched on the side lamp and made loud noises trying to wake me up. The moment I moved, he asked in a taunting tone, "Every woman loves two men, huh? What did you mean by that?"

I ignored him not wanting to start any conversation which could culminate into an argument, ruin my sleep and peace of mind.

He continued, "I thought you still loved me. Am I not providing you and the kids with everything you want? What else do you need?"

He pulled me towards himself and the expression on his face made me smirk. This did not go down well with him. In the last few years, in an attempt to force his authority over me in the garb of love, he would use sex to make up with me. He thought he was doing me a favour by this gesture and I felt that it was his attempt to feel satisfied that he was the man of the house.

Sex was just a physical act for us now. "Yoga gives me more pleasure than sex," I chuckled when Farida asked me about our intimate life. It was nothing more than an act and his arrival. I had almost forgotten what an orgasm meant or felt like.

Feelings or emotions were fading away speedily. Yet, I never said no to him. I chose to be quiet and let him have his way. I think it was because I feared his reaction if I refused or maybe I desired to make him love me again.

Between Pritam's interest in other girls and Veena's words I was losing my self-confidence. I was compared to others and told what I lacked. I started feeling that I was carrying a heavy load of emotions, sadness, confusion and rejection.

Gradually, I was realising that despite my ability to maintain a perfect and smooth image of success and grandeur in society, deep inside, I longed for love.

The void for love and respect was increasing.

The expectation of love and respect was diminishing.

Marriages are made in heaven and … in hell too.

"Radhika is getting married."

I looked up from the school book I was reading, unsure of what Pritam expected me to say at this announcement.

Sensing the change of atmosphere in the room, our elder one also looked up at Pritam and then at me. I was sitting in the children's room, helping them with their homework.

"The wedding is next week and both of us have to go," he said and left the room.

On the day of the wedding, as soon as we entered the venue Pritam said that we have to go to the bride's room to meet Radhika.

As we reached there, Radhika quickly ushered the others out of the room till just the three of us were left. He hugged her, held her hand, then kept his hand on her waist and she whispered in his ear. I could see his hand in the mirror behind them caressing her lower back till a giggle escaped her. I turned to leave, closing the door. As the gap of the door reduced, so did the distance between them.

After about twenty minutes, Pritam came downstairs and joined me in the large hall rather pleased with himself. His mood started taking a dive when Radhika arrived on the stage and could be seen smiling as she stood next to the groom.

I saw him crumple up a tissue and throw it on the floor fiercely as the couple on stage exchanged garlands amidst the merriment and light humour. Through a photographer's lens, it was the perfect shot as the couple finally managed to put garlands, give each other a side hug and look into each other's eyes lovingly with a big smile on their faces - THAT was the tipping point!

"You are so ugly and useless. What kind of a wife are you? And what is this that you are wearing? This colour does not even look good on you. I look bad because of you. You are on a mission to always spoil my mood. Do you not want me to be happy?" Pritam continued with a barrage of illogical accusations and abuses. Eventually, he decided that it was time to go home. Throughout the drive, I sat silently. There was nothing really to say or do.

As we reached home and got out of the car, he hit his toe on a stone that lay in front of the bonnet. Raging with anger, he picked it up and threw it at the windscreen. I gasped and jumped back, scared. I stood there for a while in shock, looking at the smashed screen while he walked towards the house. There could easily be a thousand cracks across the screen and yet, it held still. One poke would be enough for it to crumble. Each piece glittered under the street light. "Broken but beautiful," I thought. Ironically, it mirrored my situation.

That night I could not help but think about Radhika and Pritam. It was not that the employees had not tried to warn me about their growing intimacy. Between not wanting to create a scene and having no idea what to even say to him, I did not do anything.

Veena was always happy with Radhika. She encouraged Pritam to take Radhika shopping, go for coffee or invite her home for dinner. Every time we visited his parents' house, Radhika would also be invited. It had started looking odd at times. Especially when I was out of town and the family took her to the wedding of a family friend. Later an acquaintance showed me a photo where Pritam and Radhika were eating dinner from the same plate and Veena was sitting next to them, enjoying her food.

Once, as Pritam and I were going to his parents' house for Diwali, he spoke about the difference in our background and the similarity between his and Radhika's. While he spoke, I recalled Baba's words about how similarity of thought and character bring people together.

They did not even pretend to hide their closeness. Veena told me many times that Radhika should have been in this household instead of me. I understood that Veena was planning to bring Pritam and Radhika closer.

I was confused that if both loved each other so much and wanted to be together then why did Radhika choose to get married to someone else? I was also puzzled that if Pritam liked her then what was he doing with other women? Or for that matter, why was he still with me?

I was beginning to understand that for me, love was not enough to actually stay in any relationship. I needed trust, similar values and respect.

The next few days Pritam woke up late, was quiet at home and wanted me to accompany him to the office. Once there, he was irritated and disinterested.

After a client meeting, I was requested by an employee for a confidential meeting. As we sat down and the door was closed, she asked me if I knew why Radhika got married. When I declined, she leaned forward, lowered her voice and said, "Madam, Radhika wanted to get married to Sir and had asked him to divorce you. She also wanted to become the Director of the company and when Sir refused to give the directorship, she announced that she was getting married to this random man. Sir was very upset and threw stuff around in his cabin. They fought the whole day behind closed doors. Please do not share this with Sir or anyone else, Madam," she completed her sentence in haste when she heard a knock at the door.

As the pantry boy left after placing the coffee on my table, she continued, "Madam, Radhika was pregnant and that is why she had demanded the divorce and directorship." My mouth opened in shock as I remembered Pritam coming home late one night from the hospital and claiming that there had been an emergency. She also handed me an envelope which had the reports of an abortion.

Who you meet is predestined. Whom you retain is free will.

I had gone to Jaipur for some work where I met a well-known astrologer and *tantrik* who was an ardent Ma Durga *bhakt*.

He looked at me and said, "Child, every soul has its own journey to reach the Light and you have already experienced what millions are seeking for. Ma Durga is protecting you. She has shown herself to you. Be with her and in her when you need warmth from the Divine Mother. Nobody can dare to harm you."

Just like the meetings with His Holiness, The Dalai Lama; the blessings from the priest at my friend's house; or this meeting, omens were starting to appear every time I was stuck, felt stagnated or doubted myself. The omens would appear to bring a shift in my perspective of life. I thanked the Divine for showing me the way or giving messages when I needed them the most. Probably, it was a new beginning where I started following the omens and took small steps into an unknown territory with faith. I surrendered to the power above and with courage to cross over to a happy, peaceful and loving life.

On the way back to Delhi, I travelled by train. As I settled in my seat, I smiled politely at an older couple sitting in front. I opened *The Alchemist*, which I had been reading since the previous night. I was quite engrossed in the book and did not realise when someone joined us. "Hello," I heard a man take the seat next to me. I looked up briefly to return the greeting.

"I am going to Delhi. How about you?" he asked.

"Same, Delhi," I responded, going back to my book.

He started talking to the couple sitting across and I did not pay much attention until hearty laughter distracted me. Soon, instead of focusing on the book, my attention drifted to the conversation around.

I heard laughter again and it made me smile. I paused.

Slowly, I looked up to see who this person was, an unfamiliar kind of wave unfolding inside me. I wanted to be a part of this conversation, to share my thoughts too but I was hesitant. He was handsome and seemed to have a wonderful and carefree persona.

"You have a lovely smile. I do apologise for distracting you from your book with our conversation. We will try to tone it down," he said. I had not realised till then that I was staring at him and I blushed at being caught.

That is when I noticed him. Like, really noticed him. He had hazel-coloured eyes and I sensed a slight accent when he spoke English. His Hindi was perfect, though. He was eloquent and seemed intelligent.

Soon, I closed my book and became part of the conversation. He noticed my book and exclaimed, "The Alchemist! Great book. I have come to believe its line that 'when you truly desire something, the universe conspires to help you achieve it."

I did not realise when we reached Delhi. "So soon?" I thought. We had a wonderful discussion that ranged from food, movies and places to see around the world to the economic situation of India.

I had missed such engaging and mind-tickling conversations where a different opinion led to more insight. Healthy, soulful arguments which give equal right to one's point of view and are received respectfully were missing in my married life. The exchange with this stranger felt like home.

It seems that over time, people have lost the skills to discuss and argue. I had always learnt that just because someone is right, it does not mean that the other is wrong. As Voltaire had famously said, "I disapprove of what you say, but I will defend to the death your right to say it."

I wanted to talk more but the journey had ended. "It was a pleasure meeting you. Here is my card," he said. I took the card and we went our separate ways. As I sat in the car to go home, I realised that we never exchanged our names. I laughed loudly. "Mr. Hazel Eyes, thank you for today. Everything happens for a reason. If meeting you again is for our betterment, it will surely happen and that is when I will get to know your name. Till then, I will keep your card and you will remain a wonderful mystery," I thought to myself as I kept the card in my bag, without seeing his name.

When we lose the connect with our normal, abnormal starts happening.

I replayed the journey from the train in my head multiple times in the days that followed. For a third person, there was nothing extraordinary in this exchange but for me, it left a deep impact. It was after long that someone spoke to me as an equal on varied topics, giving me a chance to present my thoughts and appreciate the insights. This exchange would not have made an impact on a 20-year-old Tara because that was normal for her, but it was not anymore. I realised what I had lost along the way. All conversations at home were dominated around my inabilities as a wife, daughter-in-law and mother, and in social gatherings on unamusing jokes about marriages, affairs and gossip.

I picked up the card twice in the first week to see his name or save his number but stopped for I knew that if I did, I would want to call and talk to him. I tried hard to keep the memory of that beautiful conversation alive for a few months but eventually the routine of guests, drinks, parties, anger, silence and work occupied the space and dominated my mind. Slowly, the glimmer of hope started losing its shine.

A month later, I went to the Kayakalp Ayurvedic Centre in Palampur, Himachal Pradesh, for a week's course. It was a much-needed mental, emotional and physical rejuvenation.

I wanted to be at peace and in the present for as long as I could. On my way back to Delhi, while waiting at the boarding gate of Kangra Airport, I bought *Angel Medicine* by Doreen Virtue and *Am I a Hindu?* by Ed Viswanathan. As I opened the first book I felt the aura of His Holiness, the Dalai Lama. I looked around the waiting area and let out a small laugh as meeting him again would have been too good to be true. It is considered a blessing if you have met His Holiness even once in your lifetime and I was truly grateful for having had that opportunity. That interaction had left quite a profound impression on me. Dismissing the thought from my mind, I continued reading till boarding was announced.

Once inside the aircraft, I settled into my seat and waited patiently as they seemed to be running late. Just when I looked at my watch for the time, the air hostess announced, "Ladies and gentlemen, there is a slight delay as His Holiness, the Dalai Lama, and his entourage are travelling with us. Thank you for your patience."

I could not believe it. I could not stop smiling as I saw him entering the plane. Once we took off, I went to meet him and requested him to sign my copy of *Angel Medicine*. I shared that after our last meeting I had been travelling and finding myself. "The journey continues," I told him. He smiled. I also mentioned how much I loved reading his book, *The Art of Happiness*. It was full of clear, simple, and practical wisdom and how beautifully he addressed many issues that we face in daily life, especially where he talked about *Karma*.

It said, "In mentioning *Karma*, here I think it is important to point out and understand that due to one's misunderstanding of the Doctrine of *Karma*, there is a tendency to blame everything on *Karma* and try to exonerate oneself from the responsibility or from the need to take personal initiative. One could quite easily say, 'This is due to my past *Karma*, my negative past *Karma*, what can I do? I am helpless.' This is a totally wrong understanding of *Karma*. *Karma* means 'action'. It is a very active process. There is always a choice to initiate what you truly want to do and bring change, positive change. So, *Karma* should not be understood in terms of passive, static kind of force, but rather, should be understood in terms of an active process. This indicates that there is an important role for the individual agent to play in determining the course of the Karmic process."

He listened to me with a smile and blessed me. Going back to my seat, I remembered some of his quotes that I loved.

* "If you think you are too small to make a difference, try sleeping with a mosquito."
* "Everything you do has some effect, some impact."
* "Happiness is not something ready-made, it comes from your own action."

Some meetings hold mystery and others create

On a beautiful December afternoon, I was supposed to meet a school friend for lunch. The sky was cloudy and a soft breeze hinted at the probability of rain. My friend was running late and called to apologise. "It is such a romantic weather and you are making me wait. Not fair," I laughed as I teased her. "Come fast!"

In all honesty, I did not mind waiting. I loved the serenity of the place, surrounded by plants; the weather only added to the charm. Suddenly, Mr. Hazel Eyes appeared in front of me. I gasped. How…? Quickly, I fixed my expression and invited him to sit.

"I am not sure if you are happy to see me. You are smiling but you had a horrified look on your face. It was a strange combination," he said.

"Oh no! I was just surprised. I am glad to see you again. Do not look so sceptical. I am genuinely happy to see you," I said as he let out a beautiful laugh. "How are you?" I asked earnestly.

We spoke for a few minutes and I felt as if I had found a long-lost friend. There was instant comfort and we decided to meet for dinner the week after.

"By the way, I never got your name," said Mr. Hazel Eyes.

"Tara. And yours?"

"Shiv."

My heart skipped a beat. Was this a sign? My only confidante, guide and saviour, especially in the last few years, had been Lord Shiva. I knew this could not be a coincidence. "They do not happen so easily to me, remember!" I mused.

Maybe my Shiva had sent Shiv to be the friend I desperately needed but then dismissed the thought.

"See you next week," he smiled and waved as he made his way out, leaving me to my thoughts.

I love myself as I am in the moment
Without conditions, without reason.

The day I was supposed to meet Shiv, Pritam announced in the morning that he was leaving for Dehradun. Every day, since Radhika's wedding, he had been either "extremely busy" or "very angry". He packed his bags and left without a goodbye, as had become his ritual. At least today, he informed us that he was going on a trip for four days.

In the evening, I was thrilled and confused. I changed five outfits. Eager and nervous, I reached the restaurant and there he was, smiling and happy as I had seen him on the train. It was a beautiful restaurant and I was impressed with his selection as I enjoyed trying different cuisines. Being a passionate cook myself, I was particular about the taste and presentation of the dish, ambience and the table I sat at.

As we chatted, live music started playing and we both sang along with the song, one of the hit numbers of Kishore Kumar. Suddenly, something struck me and I pulled myself back. What was I doing? Was he married? I was married and this was not a business meeting. What was this and why was I here with this stranger?

I excused myself and barged into the washroom. I waited for the girl to exit and locked the door. Facing the mirror, I saw the internal turmoil reflect on my face. What was I doing here? Was I out of my mind?

Nervous of these foreign feelings, I almost heard my stomach curdling. I knew I was attracted to this unknown man who I had met on the train and knew nothing about. My heart told me to stay but my brain told me to run.

My heart was fluttering but I wondered if I was supposed to feel guilty about this new feeling? I covered my face and promised myself to have just one drink and leave in exactly half an hour.

Three hours later, I was still there. The music was soulful unlike the loud cacophony I disliked. The talk flowed from politics to music to Krishna Consciousness. This handsome man had the curiosity of a child, energy of a youngster and wisdom of an elder.

Something told me to leave or else I would never be able to. I bid him goodbye and rushed out like Cinderella towards my car. It was magical. It was the moment I had waited for, for years… And it was here…

He sent a polite message, "It was great meeting you. Good music, laughter and endless topics of discussion - I had missed these. Take care." It was as if he echoed my feelings.

"Nothing lasts, nothing is finished and nothing is perfect."
- Wabi-Sabi Philosophy

For the next few days, I got busy with nothings. I avoided thinking about Shiv and the time we spent together. Usually, I would tell a dear friend everything but this time, I did not. I wanted to keep this feeling to myself and not share it with anyone.

After a week, he asked me out for coffee. It was eleven in the morning. The children had gone to school and Pritam was at the office. I got ready and reached the café in ten minutes. I knew I was getting into trouble. Yet, I indulged my heart. Deep down, I knew that I liked him and was getting pulled towards him.

It was something more than just physical attraction. There was an instant connection. He spoke to me as an equal - someone worthy of time and attention. This is what I had wanted all along, respect and honesty.

It would be wrong to say that I did not have any good memories with Pritam. We had our fair share of merriment and joy. He tried his best and I, mine but somewhere along the way, our love seemed to have faded. Every day I held on to some hope for I, or probably both of us, did not want to give up. I knew the day I gave up, I would not look back. I would fight till the end for the one I loved. If he did not love me anymore, I trusted him to be honest with me and respectfully let go of the relationship. If he was still in this relationship, it must be because he still loved me.

When I was in the third year of my college, a group of six girls, including me, were sitting in the lawn enjoying the winter sun. The conversation started with assignments and moved on to boyfriends, marriage and expectations. Everyone shared what they hoped for in their marriage and from their partner. Some wanted a luxurious lifestyle, others a big house or travelling around the world. I wanted happiness, peace and respect. It may seem weird, a holier-than-thou statement, but the only thing I ever wanted was a life-partner with whom I could converse, listen to and enjoy the simple pleasures of life - like my parents. For me, their simple, honest and joyful living was nothing less than a luxurious life. Their romance with life and between themselves excited me.

With Shiv, I felt happy and alive. I had started smiling more and laughing again. I did not mind the small ignores and insults at home because at heart I felt valued again.

I visited Farida after two months and could not stop talking about Shiv. Farida was happy to see me happy. "Am I betraying Pritam?" I asked her.

In her ten years of experience as a counsellor, Farida had met many and listened to hundreds. She rarely became close to anyone as psychology teaches empathy with disconnection and non-attachment with clients. For the first time, she prayed for Tara's safety and happiness because by now she understood that Pritam came from a dysfunctional family.

He was a control freak, a trait probably inherited from his mother. She knew that the twinkle in Tara's eyes, the return of her smile and genuine laughter would not go unnoticed by Pritam. The girl was happy and its potential consequences scared Farida. It would take him just a moment to draw her back into the toxic loop.

Some stay even after they leave.

I was working with new energies. I started painting again, read more books than ever and stopped wearing make-up to mask myself. I resumed exercising, meeting people, enjoying parties and watching movies. I felt good. I felt like myself.

Pritam noticed the change in me. He was a keen observer and a shrewd businessman. He may have been busy but he kept a sharp eye on me, especially since an astrologer had told him years ago that all his good luck and growth came to him because of me. If we ever broke up, he would lose almost everything. He had been cautious since then to ensure that I was his.

At work, the guest list for the office's annual function was being made. Pritam gave me the list and asked if I wanted to add anyone's name to the list.

I wrote down "Shiv".

Like every year, the function was celebrated at a fancy venue with official clients, professionals, staff and a few high-profile friends. The evening had live music, dance, drinks, games and fun activities.

Pritam and Shiv were introduced. Cards were exchanged and the former was happy as Shiv was working in a Fortune

500 company.

After about three months Shiv gave a huge contract to our company. Pritam was happy and decided on another celebration. We all started meeting together. He was okay if I met Shiv for coffee or a meal.

Shiv and I were basking in a childlike romance. Just like two kids playing on the beach, unaware and unconcerned, busy making sandcastles. We would surprise each other, and go for plays and movies with or without Pritam. We joined courses and made our own group of friends.

I did not want to share about this with anyone.

I remembered a quote by Kahlil Gibran:

"Travel and tell no one,
Live a true love story and tell no one,
Live happily and tell no one,
People ruin beautiful things."

There was peace and joy, outside and within me.

Alas, too much silence may be a warning of an approaching storm. After six months, due to some professional differences, the contract between the two companies ended.

The storm had arrived.

Within a week Pritam asked me not to meet Shiv anymore. "Why? What happened?" I asked.

"I do not need to give you any explanation. You are not meeting him again. He is not good for us anymore," he replied.

Now every time Shiv asked me to meet him, I would give some excuse and decline. It is not like we used to meet every day but we had the solace and comfort of knowing that the other was there.

I was becoming restless and sad with each missed call or refusal to catch up as I was losing a dear friend. Eventually, he stopped calling, probably confused at this sudden detachment. He must have sensed something was amiss but it was not his place to interfere. I was always over-apologetic on the phone, feeling helpless and guilty for doing this to Shiv. I was used to feeling guilty or made to feel so but I did not want Shiv to be the collateral damage.

At home, Pritam started demanding my attention. The man who was always "extremely busy" and still spent hours locked up in his room with Radhika for special discussions, suddenly started reaching home before time. The man, who had showed that his sexual appetite was negligible was now making love many times a day. Not only this, he also made sure that I was without a mobile phone and kept busy 24x7. He hovered around me and I came to know that he got all my mobile bills checked as well.

I was hit by a bolt since I was literally held captive by Pritam. Unable to bear this, I confided in Farida, "It has been months since I met Shiv. I miss him a lot. Every time I eat something tasty, I want to share it with him. Even when I read something new, I want to call and tell him about it. I miss his voice and the songs he sang beautifully." I did not know how or why I started howling as if mourning a loss.

Even at times when I cannot see, I trust the hands that are holding me.

Pritam now took me to office every day, made me sit in front of him the whole day, asked me to cook for him every evening and then visit his foul-mouthed and ill-mannered mother who misbehaved every time and left no chance to insult me directly or indirectly. Months passed and I often wondered why I was enduring this pain and suffering. Probably I wanted it to push me to the maximum limit, break me down enough to break through.

Pritam showed that he was taking care of me well and giving me his full attention and time. He forgot that love does not mean strangulation, not giving the other any space or controlling the other. His way of showing care and concern meant having me at home, with him and for him, as he wanted.

One morning, I told Pritam that I needed to shop for the house and myself. I left my mobile phone with him and went with his driver. There was little I could do without my phone and under the watchful eye of his driver and so, he agreed as if he was doing me a favour. I had started telling these lies just to be able to get out and have a moment to myself. I chose the market that had my favourite café. I got off at the parking lot and quickly made my way to the café. I always enjoyed sitting by the big window looking across the pavement, watching the world go by and stray dogs fast asleep after their long night shift.

Lost in my thoughts with warm coffee cupped in my hands, I felt as if someone was looking at me. Taking my eyes away from the window I turned my head and saw Shiv standing in front of me. Instinctively, I stood up, hugged him and started crying. This was the first time we had hugged since we met.

Confused, he did not know what had happened or how to react. I had been avoiding him, then called him suddenly only to tell him that we could not meet and now this?

He hugged me reluctantly and slowly the grip became firm. I knew he wanted to hold me in his arms but always refrained himself as I was married. Today, he mustered up the courage to hug me back and hold me tightly.

For the next few minutes I spoke, cried, laughed, cried again and told him everything - the love, hurt, abuses, struggles and the success. I did not let go of his hand and he listened, taking it all in.

It appeared he could gather my fear, hope, trust, and helplessness to leave everything and run away and yet, not be able to. I did not know what to do and he did not know what to say. Every time I thought of my children, I became silent and chose my enslavement.

Both Shiv and I were nervous, not because Pritam had told me not to meet him but because we did not know what we felt for each other. We both wondered if this was love. Whatever it was, we did not want to think about it or even acknowledge it for we knew that we might not meet again.

A part of me knew that I should be afraid in case Pritam found out that I had spoken to Shiv, let alone met him but I could not even muster up courage to feel fearful. I was just tired.

Shiv and I were together in that moment, not hoping or wishing anything for the future. We were just there.

"Everything that happens once can never happen again. But everything that happens twice will surely happen a third time." - Paulo Coelho

It had been almost six months since I met Shiv at the café. I had stopped crying under the shower these days and had lost a lot of weight. I did not feel the same and was living each day as it dawned and with each dusk it faded. Days were fine as I kept myself occupied but nights were difficult. At times, I lay in bed awake and at other times I slept with the help of a sleeping pill.

I discovered that my body and mind shut down when I was away from my soulful living and equilibrium. I got back to my meditations, and started seeking harmony, balance and managing the mind.

It is interesting how we choose to shut down our deepest hurts and pains. We hide it somewhere in our memory and cover it up with extra add-ons like toppings on a pizza. Forgetting deliberately is a prerequisite to being forgetful. During the spiritual courses I observed how I was now familiar with shutting myself. Slowly I started getting forgetful about the smallest of things, events, and even my needs and wants. Conscious numbing - where we choose to bury the pain or become insensitive towards people, situations or words which hurt us.

"Being forgetful under shock is called dissociative (psychogenic) amnesia which stems from emotional shock or trauma," Farida told me.

Pritam and I started visiting different cities and countries, either for work or vacations and he always told me that he was doing it for me. In reality, it reduced my chance of meeting Shiv and allowed him to supervise me all the time.

Life continued and we started living our "normal life" yet again. Two rights in a wrong partnership.

My mobile phone was returned after screening all messages and pictures, and deletion of many contact numbers.

"Do not lose heart, Tara. I am sure Pritam is stuck too," Farida said during a session. "He probably did not know if you were too meek, over understanding, forgiving or just scared when it came to his outbursts or lies. He neither had clarity about you nor himself. He was with you because it was correct for him, convenient for him and you were his safety net. He knew you would always be there for him, for money cannot buy loyalty. He feared loss - of any kind - and the astrologer's predictions about his loss if you left him scared him. Yet, he wanted to be with you and with Radhika and others. His needs and wants were clashing. He needed you but he wanted and desired Radhika.

It is said that if you have truly loved someone once, you have the capacity to love and you will surely have someone to love you again. First start loving yourself, young lady," said Farida.

"Being deeply loved by someone gives you strength,
While loving someone deeply gives you courage." - Lao Tzu

I was attending courses in whatever subject or skill I liked, the majority being on spirituality. I was grateful to Pritam as he never interfered in my journey of spirituality, in fact he often encouraged me to continue pursuing it. He was satisfied as I was busy with my "little hobby", as he called it, not realising that it was leading me towards diverse realisations, opening up the Universe and its many possibilities.

Interestingly, I was introduced to silence at a young age. Maa used to encourage Bhaiya and me to close our eyes and look inwards. At that age, I wondered what was inwards and slowly realised that everything was inside me. I understood that peace was energy and being peaceful was energetic, and since then silence became precious to me. I entered the meta-physical realm because of Pritam and along the way many situations were thrown my way to challenge my inner strength and untap my true self. Spirituality answered many of my questions. It also brought to the surface older memories, pains and pleasures.

When Pritam and I started our journey together, we had similarities. Over time, rather than fostering those, differences were added. We were both caring, travelled together, loved hosting people at home and always made sure everyone was comfortable in our company. We worked as a team. Pritam trusted me with the house like I trusted him with the office.

Both of us worked hard and waded through the early challenges of marriage and started our business, all by ourselves. We were proud of our togetherness. Eventually, instead of strengthening our relationship and concentrating on each other, our teamwork and partnership developed cracks. Just the shell remained.

The small shift in perspective shifted our attention from love and acceptance towards differences and dissatisfaction. I probably know now when the crack happened but Pritam and I were too young to handle it.

> *Dear Diary,*
>
> *When Pritam committed the mistake for the first time, he was not stopped. Maybe I should have done something then. I never involved my parents because neither did I want to trouble them nor did I ever think matters would get out of hand. It was the same when his mother misbehaved with me for the first time. Maa and Baba had warned me about this marriage. How could I go to them now? I should have gone earlier and asked for help. It is too late now. They may become collateral damage the way Shiv has become. I cannot let my parents know anything. Pritam will make their lives miserable and sever all ties with them. I will have to handle it on my own. I have no other alternative.*
>
> *- Stuck in between*
> *Tara*

Pritam was happy when his detectives reported that my destinations were limited to the house, office and workshops, and all my meetings were as per the names he had pre-approved. Shiv was no longer in the picture. Despite that, his insecurity made him instruct the detectives to continue watching me. He had found a way to keep me busy, yet, on a leash. I realised that a year in our life was divided into three phases.

Four months were dominated by arguments, insults, lies and separate involvements.

Two months were dedicated to a tense negative environment with silent treatment and abusive behaviour that affected the entire family.

Finally, six months were our happy, energetic and productive time. Here we would be together as a family, have friends over, enjoy and have vacations.

Intent, willingness and action change the course of destiny on the basis of free will.

It is said if you want to change your outlook then you have to edit and expand your circle of friends. You become the company you keep. Your actions are motivated more by what you see than what you perceive.

As I learnt different healing modalities I heard, saw and felt the pain and sufferings of many. I found resemblance with some while with others it instilled a feeling of gratitude.

I deciphered the difference between pain and suffering. We all know that pain is inevitable and suffering is a choice. Everyone goes through pain in their lives yet not everyone chooses to suffer. Everything starts in the subconscious mind till it makes a home there. The choices we make are also a reflection of the soul's need. We may have a void and to make it up we fill it with suffering, or acts of over-giving or receiving.

The moment the realisation of the cause for the suffering occurs, the choice or the test of free will appears to move out of the suffering. What matters most is the intent to shift, followed by the willingness to make the move and finally, the execution of the intent.

The awareness of the cause itself is a step towards self-healing. It is rightly said, "Seeing is healing," because we often blindfold ourselves and tie our own hands. The moment we untie our hands, open our eyes, and look at it with full awareness, healing starts.

The journey had always been more important than the destination and in this case the internal journey was significant as the destination was the same for all. I began to experience the depth and height of the connection, to be linked with the higher vibrations, well-tuned with the spirit world yet connected to my roots of existence. For me, learning was meaningful only when it was incorporated in daily life, in this Earth reality.

During one of these experiences, I journeyed into my mother's womb. I saw myself as peaceful, strong and joyful, clad in a saffron cloth. During the delivery, there was a dim light.

Maa always asked about my experiences in class - what I learnt rather than what was being taught. That day, when I shared the experience with her, she smiled and told me that while she was carrying me, she used to read texts by Swami Vivekananda and hence, I saw the saffron cloth.

When I asked about the dim lights, I was told that the gynaecologist and obstetrician preferred dimness for natural deliveries at night in the labour room.

Knowing is a pure form of consciousness.

Upbringing and environment play a vital role in one's outlook. The relationship between the parents, how they behave at home and outside, and how they bring up their children defines the child's thoughts and actions in life.

The primary relationship is between the mother and the child and it lays the foundation for their future relationships. It is seen that the way the mother raises her son reflects on his relationship with other women in his life. If you have a strong relationship, stemming from trust and love then that is what it shall be later in his life. If there is fear, insecurity, disturbance, irritation or expectations, that is replicated in the forthcoming bonding too.

A woman raises her daughter to complete her incomplete dreams and son to complete her wishes. The son is raised with the fear of losing control and the daughter is raised with the fear of retaining pride. We learn fear from a very early stage of our life. It is like a family heirloom, carried forward with each generation. Along with fear, shame, guilt and ego come in a package deal.

Fear on the part of the mother forces her from letting the boy become a complete man. A man remains a boy or a half-man to live fully and fulfilling as an independent being yet he is expected to be the provider for safety, even if he is not ready emotionally. A girl matures to become a woman and is expected to carry on the role and responsibility with maturity even if she is not ready.

In a patriarchal society, a father's relationship with the child is intriguing. The man is not a natural caretaker. This instinct comes organically with individuals who have higher feminine energy. He sees himself as a provider and giver, who is stern and talks only when required and expects a lot in return. He may want his son to follow his footsteps to become like him and in future, take care of them when they are older. With a daughter, he provides everything with no expectation in return. He gives his daughter's hand in marriage to the man whom he trusts to take care of her.

Sometimes, I felt bad for Pritam as he had a disturbing equation with his mother. I did understand and empathise but I also knew that it always depended on a person what they chose to become. One can either learn from their own or other's mistakes and not repeat them or choose to turn a blind eye and commit the same blunder again and again. It is easier to say that behaviour or action is the effect of *Karma* from past lives or the current life's past experience but the fact remains that you always have a choice to change the track and act towards a desired path.

It is to understand that we are governed and blessed by the supreme intelligence and we have progressed because of the need to question and find answers.

The Theory of Probability says that, "The outcome of a random event cannot be determined before it occurs, but it may be any one of several possible outcomes. The actual outcome is considered to be determined by chance." It is seen in card games, sports matches, tossing of the coin, and even for predicting the weather. In each success there is a probability of fifty percent failure.

I felt that if Pritam was smart enough to run a business, knew which car to purchase, where to go for a holiday, understood human psychology and put it in use for his work, and also knew from a young age which actions of his mother were wrong, then he surely knew how to behave with me, his wife. It was not possible for him to plead innocence and feign ignorance. It was evident that these were well-calculated actions.

This only went on to reinforce that each one of us is born with a peculiar essence and archetype, and we act according to that. Baba had talked about it once, "The inner essence or *vriti* never changes. We all are born with certain individual traits and they are well-seeded in each of us." He had simplified it by stating an example that a mango tree will always bear mangoes and not apples. In certain rare cases, individuals have been known to change their *vriti*. Here, the Theory of Probability does not work.

It requires heightened awareness, strong determination and constant conscious and consistent efforts for a soul to alter its *vriti* or the course of action. That is when soul plans are also altered and '*Aham Brahmasmi*' comes alive to its magnificent form and we can say that, "I am the creator of my own destiny."

The soul journeys made me realise my inner essence. I could see this in my children also. Both were born of the same parents, lived and experienced similar situations yet they responded differently to a situation. By then, I had become aware of the mystery of Soul Contracts wherein each soul made a contract with another for its learning. Whatever was left in a lifetime, those desires, lessons and unfulfilled promises were carried forward to the next birth. This continued until understanding finally dawned upon the person.

Here, I also learnt the difference between the soul and spiritual journey. Everything contains a soul. It is on the spiritual journey through self-evolution, learning and moving towards the ultimate enlightenment, the *moksha*. The soul chooses the womb, parents, place and family structure to live as an extension of the learning from the past birth which is carried forward to the present birth and continues till its purpose is not fulfilled.

Right from the choice of womb to the fate of death is carved by the soul plan. Yet, there is a window which opens now and then, a knock on the door, soft or loud, where we can choose. The Universe always offers an opportunity to liberate ourselves from the clutches of the usual, the suffering or an undesired path. It gives us an opening to exert free will.

Time and again, I heard and talked about choices. Probably my subconscious mind was preparing me to make one. Everything was alive and connected. It was like knowing the difference between the soul and the spirit. There was soul in everything. It travelled across births and yet was constant. The spirit was the connection to the Almighty. We felt spirited when connected. We varied in our spirits. The soul had a spiritual journey to complete. We were on our own spiritual paths but everyone's destination was the same, meeting the source, the Light.

I realised that I had been a visionary more than a dreamer. I always created a vision for fulfilment. I often wondered why I never dreamt like others. When I was calm and grounded, visions would just appear, show me some omen or give signs, and fly past.

I read the *Bhagavad Gita*, Rhonda Bryne's *The Secret*, and works by Osho, Sri Ramana Maharshi, Mahatma Gandhi, Brian Weiss, Paulo Coelho, Elif Shafak, and other such authors and books. I loved how the wise explained everything with such simplicity. I agree with Albert Einstein's words that, "If you cannot explain something simply then you have not understood it completely."

I preferred the simple way of communication without the need to use extra or complicated words. I believed that language is only a tool to communicate and cross barriers for understanding; like money is a tool to live life comfortably. Leonardo da Vinci puts it well when he says, "Simplicity is the ultimate sophistication."

"A cloud does not know,
Why it moves in just such a direction,
And at such a speed.
It feels an impulsion…
This is the place to go now
But the sky knows
The reason and the patterns behind all clouds
And you will know, too,
When you lift yourself high enough to see beyond horizons."
- Richard Bach

The Divine throws many challenges at you to test your determination towards your soul purpose.

A bomb dropped. Pritam had asked Veena and Dhyanchand to shift in with us.

Was he out of his mind? Did he not know what he was doing? Had he gone crazy? I was furious. Of all the things he did, I never imagined he would do this. He hated his mother, who in turn hated me. I never felt more betrayed. I knew that this was the worst mistake he could commit. My head, heart and instincts told me that this was a bad idea - for everyone. I wanted peace but was hit with a thunderstorm.

We argued, fought and before I could even hold myself together, a blue truck screeched in front of our house. "*Buri nazar wale tera muh kaala* (phrase used to ward off evil eye)," was written in the front of the truck, along with a black face and black strings hanging from it.

In the next three hours our furniture was pushed aside, belongings nudged and squeezed into corners as his parents' things entered through doors, windows and the terrace. The open spaces were crammed up.

Within days, silence was replaced by mistrust and accusations. The constant criticism and suffocation I had felt in the first week after marriage had returned. The only difference was that I could trust Pritam then. This time, hell was invited into our home.

Eyebrows were raised, words mocked and there were more questions than answers.

"Why is this person coming to the house?"

"Who are you talking to on the phone?"

"Why is your head not covered in front of us?"

"What is the driver's salary?"

"Why is the house help watching television?"

"How can you sleep till 7:00 A.M.?"

"Why are you sleeping with your doors closed?"

"How dare you leave the house without our permission?"

"You are supposed to sit with us. Why did you go to your friend's house for dinner?"

They started asking questions about the income and monitored the expenditure - from the quantity of food and groceries, the salaries of the staff to the money I spent on household expenditure. They wanted to control everything.

Once again, I was given a list of instructions. Dhyanchand got them printed and framed. This time, the only addition was a small list that was prepared for Pritam also.

For Tara :

1. Wake up at 4:00 A.M.

2. Have a bath and enter the kitchen

3. Finish dusting the house before everyone comes to the breakfast table

4. Eat after everyone has finished

5. Then clean the dining table and kitchen

6. Go to sleep only after the in-laws have retired for the night

7. There is no need for women to read or study too much

8. No guests or parties at home

9. Seek permission to step out of the house

10. Watching television is not allowed without prior permission

11. Children should not make any noise

12. Your parents and relatives cannot come without prior permission

For Pritam:

1. All finances are to be discussed with father

2. All expenditure will be taken care of by mother

3. Parents should be made partners in the Company

4. Travel and personal expenses will be sanctioned by the parents

5. Seek permission before any transaction or action

6. No friends or hosting parties without prior permission

Fights started taking place, tempers rose and the children were ignored. DC wanted to control the business and Veena the house.

While one couple was content as they were getting closer to their goal, the other was crumbling. Earlier, despite our problems, we were keeping our boat afloat. Now, it seemed as if a hole had been drilled into the boat. More water was coming in than we could take out. It was tiring and wearisome. I did not know how long I would be able to stand up to this as they had put a stop to my spiritual workshops, the one thing that had kept me going was also taken away from me.

As my despair increased so did Pritam's and he tried to reason with me. He assured me that he would speak to his parents and I would be allowed to attend classes again.

I contacted healers, psychics, priests and astrologers. All of them cautioned me against Veena and DC. Some even told me to do whatever I could to send them back as they had the capacity to throw me out of my own house. "You are surrounded by danger. They will devour you if you let them stay in your house," I was told. One astrologer warned me bluntly to move out of my own house to save my life.

There was little I could do. They had entered. The abuse had begun and toxicity had started taking shape. I was made to feel guilty for the smallest of things. It is said that guilt, fear, shame and ego demarcate, and decide the boundaries of any relationship.

It is not that Pritam would not fight with his parents yet he would forget that if his parents cared for him, they would have cared to create a balance rather than a rift between us.

Fear was galloping back to me at an unbelievable speed.

Words can be deceitful, Actions can be doubtful, Patterns of behaviour are reliable.

Patterns form habits, habits affect character, character influences thoughts, thoughts create words, words define actions, and actions become a pattern. To break this loop, we need to change our thoughts.

Within two months Veena started a huge fight. This time, she dragged my parents into it. Until that day, I had never retaliated no matter what Veena, DC or even Pritam said against me but I could not tolerate her speaking ill about Maa and Baba. The moment she took their names, I told her to "keep them out of it".

"Why? Why should I keep them out of it?" she asked.

I kept quiet. I knew I should not have spoken. Those five words revealed my weak point to her and she was bound to use it against me.

"What happened? Why are you quiet now?" she continued.

Just then, Pritam entered the room.

"What do you want from me, Tara? Why are you threatening me? I do not know why I even bothered to come here to help you both. Clearly you do not like me and I have taken all the insults you have thrown my way till now, but today you accuse me and threaten me like this?" she said.

"Pritam, I am very sorry. I think I should go. I cannot even imagine my prestige being attacked like this. I never wanted to have to tell you this but today your wife has threatened me."

"What?" I was stumped. "I just asked you to not insult my parents. Please do not lie."

Pritam had told me how she changed faces, especially when it came to his Dadi but I never expected it to be this swift. I was so surprised that I did not know what to say. She kept talking so fast, I felt as if I got swept into a tornado, unable to escape or control anything. I knew something bad would happen. I could sense it.

"Now, she is calling me a liar, Pritam." Veena continued, "In your house, I have no say or standing. Should your father and I go and live in an old age home? Maybe, I should call some friend or relative and stay with them for a few days before we decide where to go from here."

"Mom, please!" Pritam finally spoke.

"Really Pritam? You are going to take her side now?"

I could see her getting angry.

"I guess this is it. You really are throwing me out and choosing this girl over me? I ask you one last time and you better think it through before answering - who is more important to you, me or her?" she almost spat out the words, fury evident in her eyes.

"Tara please apologise to my mother," Pritam turned around to face me.

"But I did not do anything wrong," I fumbled.

"TARA," he yelled.

"But…"

Pritam slapped me.

It had taken me almost three years and many workshops, numerous personal sessions and solo travels to bring balance back into my life. One stroke and all of it came crumbling down. Of all the things he had said to me or done, I could not find any justification for the slap.

I stood there in shock. I could not feel any emotion.

I just stood there, empty from within.

That was the first time Pritam raised his hand on me but that day, I saw evil in his eyes, eyes that burned with anger. Were the eyes really a window to the soul? Did I marry and trust a man who held so much hate and negativity within him for me? His eyes resembled his mother's that evening.

There was complete silence. For the people who always had something to say, this was a first. I could not even look up to see the relief flash in Veena's eyes. I neither had the strength nor the will to retort. I felt paralytic. My soul had gone into shock, rendering me motionless.

Pritam told me to apologise to her by touching her feet.

"Can you not hear what I said?" he shouted.

I did what I was told.

He stormed out of the house and I went to our room. The scars were increasing and the strength diminishing. Each time a portion of my soul was breaking apart. Till now, he had thrown tantrums, broken television screens, phones, windscreen and other household items. Was I just another thing for him?

He had slapped me. Every time I thought that this was the worst that could happen, Pritam surpassed himself.

Something shifted between us. We both felt it.

The next few days he made attempts to get intimate. I did not know if it was an attempt to reclaim his manhood or an apology. If it was the latter, then he really had a twisted sense of shame and guilt.

Each soul has its own song,
Some remember to sing,
Some forget.
Every song, echoes the desire of the soul journey,
Each soul has a purpose,
Some move towards it,
And for some the purpose curates and creates the way.

It is the conditioning of the mind and body that we come back to. Having a similar reaction for similar events is a natural inclination.

We fear to tread the unknown and so choose to react in the same way again and again. It is difficult to expect a different outcome when we repeat a similar reaction. Nobody has the power to force us to do something without our approval. Even if it is an action we disapprove of and still execute, it is our choice. Whatever reasoning or excuses we give are just for our own peace of mind. The fact remains that it only happens through our acceptance to act.

As you read these lines, the logical mind will immediately come up with at least one situation where this can be countered. The neutral mind will find scenarios where this is applicable and the insightful mind will understand its relevance in everyday situations. For example, a person may be fearful of ghosts. It is a familiar reaction that we find convenient and so we get scared. Have you ever questioned what will happen if you decide not to get scared? Baba always said, "Why be scared of something that does not have a form? It cannot touch you nor can it affect you. Be cautious if it has an impact on you and takes form out of nothing. Otherwise, change your perception and reaction."

However, that was easier said than done. I realised that staying in this relationship was my choice, the excuses were plenty - society, children, habit and security. Pritam never forced me to stay. Our relationship was now erratic, negative, and claustrophobic with patterns of emotional and mental abuse. Still, we chose to live, love and hate. It was outside of our comfort zone to take the leap but it was convenient for us to stay together. The warmth of being together was inching towards aggression, boiling hot and growing like a volcano, though a dormant one.

I also realised that an emotion had to be within us to be able to reflect it in the outer world. No emotion can be propagated by anyone else. It was like a dormant seed and when the external environment was appropriate, it germinated. If I was fearful, it would have been hidden within me somewhere deep down. If Pritam was angry then that emotion must have been inside him, too. We could only show and give what we possess. We give what we have, we seek what we do not have.

I believed that given a choice between love and fear, love always reigned supreme and so it baffled me why Pritam would ask Veena and DC to move in with us when he had always been vocal about his dislike for his mother. One could step on shit unknowingly but this was deliberate and no words of his could justify his action.

I was attending courses to sort my thoughts and understand myself better. I became watchful and conscious. I also noticed that I was showing characteristics of playing a victim and immediately tried to avoid it for that was not who I wanted to be. During a spiritual session, I recognised that my shouts were louder than my actions.

We perceive what we want to and how we want to.

"I can do it. I am fine. I am good and happy," I convinced myself but I was not fine and I was not happy.

Repeating is good for revision but repeating with no understanding is forgotten easily. Our house, which was once a place where friends and family could visit, had now become barren. Fear had arrived and started spreading its tentacles, crawling its way through. It is said that fear travels faster than faith. I had to understand with awareness and then choose to act consciously. In my quest for answers and understanding, I went for past life regression (PLR), a technique that uses hypnosis to retrieve relevant memories from previous births to address issues which affect you in the current birth. Having learnt the technique myself, I took my time to search for a trustworthy and reputed guide for this journey.

In one of the sessions, I saw that I was a young boy who grew up to be a serious and disciplined guru. I spent all my time studying and following strict *tapasya* and prayers. People from across the world came to learn from me and till my last breath I taught *dharma* and *atma gyan* to live a fulfilling life, under a huge banyan tree.

During another session, I saw Veena as my mother and Pritam as my lover. I committed suicide because the mother did not let me meet or marry the beloved. The mother was hurt as her reputation had been tarnished.

The PLR coach guides you to apologise, write a letter or talk to the person, if identified in this lifetime. I spoke to Veena and Pritam, apologised to them and also forgave them.

"Everything will be okay in the end,
If it is not okay, it is not the end."
- John Lennon

Relationships heal us either through similarities or understanding the opposites.

I had been practising *chakra* meditation for more than five years and realised that a parallel could be drawn between different stages of a relationship with the *chakras*, the subtle energy centres in our body.

In a relationship, the first stage is of co-dependency, wherein each person is dependent on the other for money, food, shelter, and/or other basic needs of safety and security. This can be seen in the base of the spine as the root *chakra* or *muladhar.*

It is here that the seed of fear and insecurity lies. Traditionally, marriages were proposed keeping this dependency in mind. The man was considered to be the provider and the woman was responsible for converting the house into a home.

After this, comes the sacral *chakra* or *swadishthan* where the seed of creation germinates. Once the couple feels secure, they move into the dependent mode where they become intimate. Trust is formed first before letting someone come close. Once established, the couple share everything fearlessly. The man provides and the woman starts creating and together they procreate and co-create their space, food, home, children and relationships.

The moment creation happens, we have a tendency to become possessive. We start controlling what we created, be it a relationship or work. We feel that because it stems out of us, it must be controlled.

Control lies in the power centre, the solar plexus or *manipurna*, where emotions and ego reside. It is here that all boundaries are created and the dos and don'ts are defined. The relationship is still dependent and well-defined.

When all the boundaries are defined and understood with due respect to the other, the relationship has the capacity to evolve and become independent.

Once the difference in controlling others and self-control is understood, we move upward towards compassion. This stage demands a lot of work. We enter the state of love consciousness. This is the heart *chakra* or *anahat*. It is here that love, compassion and forgiveness reside. We love each other for who we and others are. We are not judgmental and respect the existence of the relationship. Forgiveness is asked, accepted and given here. Everything is equalised at the heart centre as love frees you. Yet, if and when we are controlled by our emotions, we can create havoc or heaven. It is here that we decide to either be driven by lower vibrations or function out of love and move ahead of fear, control, guilt or ego towards higher vibrations.

Once that is cleared, the relationship enters the stage of throat *chakra*, *vishuddhi*, which is the realisation point - what and how one feels about themselves in the relationship. Self-worth and communication with oneself starts from here.

This is the independent stage of the relationship where one feels safe enough to be vulnerable and communicate freely. When you feel loved and respected, you start loving and respecting yourself for your being.

You are then ready to move upwards towards the third eye, the *ajna chakra*, where the relationship starts opening. The realisation of what you have become in the relationship starts unlocking here. It is towards the reaching point of the spiritual oneness and the bond reaches the stage of wisdom. It is a beautiful stage as the understanding and realisation of a relationship reaches here after crossing over or going through insecurity, sensual attachments, control, compassion and giving and receiving of the truth.

After this, the relationship moves to the last stage, the interdependence stage and the last *chakra*, the crown or *sahasara*. The affiliation growth chart arrives at the point of union learning lessons and crossing through fear, guilt, hurt, control, doubt and reaches a stage of awareness, acceptance, trust, truth and understanding. Here, the inner twinkle appears with an extra shot of tinkle and grace from the Almighty. You are comfortable in your skin and hold the charisma to make others feel special about themselves. Breathing becomes slow, calm and the joy of togetherness is experienced in the moment.

I experienced these emotions in my marriage and realised my relationship was moving downwards. Pritam and I had started from the interdependence stage, loving and understanding each other, and somehow, slowly the relationship got stuck in the solar plexus.

During this time, I became observant of the lives of other couples, their joys and struggles.

Shreya & Amit

At twenty-seven years of age, Amit's mother had placed a photo of a girl on his desk. He was not ready for a serious relationship, let alone marriage. He wanted to study further, earn more and travel before getting married. After dinner, he reached for his laptop on the desk and the moment he picked it up, he saw the photo beneath it. He could hear his own heartbeat. He had seen her before and in that instant he knew that he wanted to have her by his side till his last breath.

They had been married for thirty-two years and lived a peaceful and interdependent life. Whenever I was in the company of this couple, I desired to experience the same bliss with my partner which I felt between Shreya and Amit. I wanted to feel this fearless, trustworthy union which was peaceful and a respectful coexistence. I wanted to live in a space where there were no deliberate and targeted arguments, showdowns, or ego boosting trips. I would often go to Shreya's home to just be there. The ambience was positive and happy. There were no games that they played nor snide remarks that were passed within the family.

Maa always said that besides what you did in a relationship or for the relationship, it was what you became in the relationship that mattered the most.

"Let there be spaces in your togetherness,
And let the winds of the heavens dance between you.
Love one another but make not a bond of love;
Let it rather be a moving sea between the shores of your souls.
Fill each other's cup but drink not from one cup.
Give one another of your bread but eat not from the same loaf."
- Kahlil Gibran

A beautiful relationship is a meditation. A relationship is nothing but a conscious effort and action. "To be in it, with it and in flow of the movements in those moments," I had written in my diary long ago.

When a relationship reaches the crown *chakra*, it becomes one, like the union of Shiva and Shakti. It merges together and generates energy to move beyond the self in the body, mind, emotion and spirit. This was what I wanted to experience in my relationship, the journey to bliss where none was better than the other yet, both were the best form of themselves. It was a relationship which not only lived but thrived. Through my eyes, Shreya and Amit had become the ideal couple.

Each was complete and chose to live, love and thrive together keeping their true essence intact. Each had the characteristics of Shiva and Shakti. Each individual was a provider and receiver in the relationship. I understood that only the completeness in oneself could fulfil the completeness in the other and that is when the relationship thrived.

The three elements that matter the most in a relationship are vibration, frequency and rhythm. I once read that when the vibes meet, there is an instant connect called Vibration Energy Harvesting. The concept is simple. Hypothetically, all vibration energy can be transformed into electrical energy and an electromagnetic field is created to let the current flow in rhythm.

Just as wavelength and frequency are related to light, they are also related to energy. Shorter wavelength and higher frequency correspond with greater energy.

Rhythm is a strong, regular, repeated pattern of movement or sound. Any given relationship formed in time, space and situation is based on these elements, to match the vibration, to be on the same frequency and it moves in the rhythm to make beautiful music to soothe the soul.

I recalled Baba's words, "Similar character of thought" and "interests unite and interests divide." I added 'intent' to interest. He used to say, "A person may get attracted to the opposite yet, similarity sustains. How one responded in a given situation reflected their character which went back to their belief system." I somehow also felt that intent and interest completed the beliefs and character.

We had learnt the simple theories in our school like, "Everything is energy and its constant feature is to flow. It can neither be destroyed nor created. It just is." "It is friction that creates heat, and one has to identify whether it is moving backwards or forwards or sidewards." "Wherever the attention goes, the flow follows. The moment it gets stuck, it has a possibility of stagnation, it has a tendency to get rusted." However, we only memorised for marks and never understood it in real life - the curse of human limitation.

I learnt the value of synthesis very early in my life. I recognised the existence of thesis and the significance of antithesis to reach the state of synthesis, the value of holding the view and the probability of having an opposite point of view were equally important to get the complete picture.

Perhaps that was why I understood and accepted the differences between Pritam and myself. That was why I, most likely, figured out the different thinking processes of Veena and now Pritam, as they descended from different vibration, frequency and character of thought.

Ritu & Sunil

Besides Shreya and Amit, I witnessed another couple's chemistry, Ritu and Sunil. They had three lovely kids and a wonderful marriage until misunderstandings caused by in-laws started drawing them apart. They started bickering, complaining and neglecting each other. The fights had begun and they began avoiding each other and formed their own definition of a relationship that was comfortable for them. Both developed their own circles of comfort to vent their frustrations. From outside, it appeared to be quiet and tense at times but they were together and everyone accepted it as it is.

Prachi & Joe

They had been married for years now and had one child. Both descended from dissimilar backgrounds. Their thoughts, reactions, beliefs and approaches were different but their marriage worked as they cared about each other. They respected the differences and slowly their love brought them closer. Joe shared that what kept any relationship alive was respect. He believed it to supersede love. Joe was sensitive about thoughts, words and actions, and Prachi was an ardent believer in fate. She accepted that whatever happened was for the good. They had stopped questioning or complaining to each other. They had their flings and attractions outside their marriage and they shared it with each other as best friends do. Besides being separate in ways of thoughts and reaction, they still chose to live together peacefully. They learnt to co-exist.

At first, it was a new arrangement for me to understand but I surrendered to reason it out as the couple was at peace. Very few make the choice to rock the boat of dissatisfaction. I had witnessed men cracking jokes on marriage and affairs, while women bickered behind their back but still both chose to live together.

Extramarital affairs, separations and ugly divorces were a part of society which I had not noticed enough to care about until now. I used to turn a blind eye and retire to my own life, safe and protected in the shackles of abusive living.

Sanjana & Abhishek

Sanjana and Abhishek were married but to someone else. Both of them and their respective spouses were friends once upon a time and then these two became closer. Fights occurred in both houses but they continued to meet. Eventually, Abhishek's wife sought a divorce. All four were now focused on their respective childrenand behaved well and civilised for the sake of the children.

Shubham

One of my friends, Shubham, recently had an ugly divorce. He had been married off at a young age but never got attached to his bride. After a few years, they separated. Both of them found other partners and married again. Everything was fine until Shubham's new wife tried to take control of his life. She used him for his green card, crushed his pride and confidence, emptied his bank account and defamed him. He had a messy separation but it was a relief when he freed himself from all the suffering.

Nisha

At one of my social meet-ups, I met Nisha who shared that she loved her husband and family but had a higher libido. She had opted for a travelling job so that she could satisfy her needs and her marriage remained intact as she respected the institution.

Priya

She had married her childhood lover and after ten years of marriage she met a woman and fell in love with her. The family was stunned and Priya moved out of her marriage and dared to live with her new partner along with her son. The husband went through denial, bargain, anger, sadness and then accepted the change. It took them time but they maintained an amicable relationship for their child's sake.

Every couple had a story. Each was right and none was wrong.

They all had their own share of love, betrayal, resentment, judgement, adjustment, compromise, understanding and ego. Each story was weaved into a variety of emotions. Every couple had built their own chemistry. No two relationships were or could be compared nor should they be. How families respond to a situation brings the members together or pulls them apart.

The spiritual workshops brought the complex and complementary bonds in view. I loved peace and free flow of the breath. For me the flow of breath became the parameter of my sense of knowing and confirmation of my existence. I realised how naïve I had been.

Dear Diary,

I wonder what is right or wrong, good or bad. Who decides what is right or wrong? For one science is good, for another poetry; for one dawn is the best time to meditate, for another it might be dusk; some value money and others relationships.

Is it right to think and fantasise about someone else other than the one who is in your arms? Is it right to be with someone who you do not love? If the latter is right, then the former cannot be wrong? Is it right to be wrong to yourself or is it wrong to be right to yourself?

Black and White

"Colours of the zebra are black and white,
Nothing more, nothing less
They all look the same
Yet, each stripe is different from the other
The contrast between the colours reflects the essence of
each being
Different, alone and merged among all

These questions gripped my attention, the metaphysical world started offering answers to some of my questions. The inner child therapy uncovered hidden emotions. Here I addressed my needs to be pampered and cared for. I acknowledged and accepted the reality, understood it, made peace with it, healed it and closed it. At least, I thought I had closed it.

I wanted to share all this with Pritam but he could neither understand nor relate to it. Instead, he felt betrayed, as if I had eloped with someone. So, I stopped sharing with him and introduced him to the spiritual world so that he grows himself, at his pace to understand what I was learning, hoping that he might understand himself and our relationship.

With the extension in knowledge and understanding, I grew from within but the atmosphere inside the house was enough to stagnate and strangulate that growth. I felt as if I was taking two steps forward and one step backward. Veena and DC subtracted the happy times, multiplied confusion, divided the family and added ill will. They were constant, never changing with similar vibrations and on a different frequency.

The festivities were getting heavier with too many expectations. Gifts were scrutinised and vacations were scorned. Pritam began to participate in his parents' game smartly, now. Everyday a new frustration was displayed. He wanted everything but on his own terms and conditions, and did not want to claim responsibility. DC had already put his foot inside the door to control the company and Veena the house. Radhika wanted to become rich and improve her social status. Pritam had everything but our bond was losing it to his pride, ego and unwillingness to untangle and declutter the disturbing elements of our lives.

Almost everything was a trigger for his anger. I remember vividly the evening when we went for my friend's birthday celebration and everyone had started dancing to retro beats. At parties, Pritam was often found on the dance floor, enjoying. That day, as the girls pulled me to the dance floor while he was sitting at the table, I could feel his eyes on me even from a distance. I asked him to join in but he refused. I could see anger in his eyes. After about two songs, he stood up from his chair, walked over to me on the dance floor and told me that we were leaving. I said my goodbyes to everyone and left, walking behind Pritam. As we sat in the car, he started yelling at me.

We reached home and he did not speak to me for the next three months on the allegation that I was having a good time while he was getting bored. It was absurd! A few months later, he again became violent and broke the television screen. His parents were standing there, watching quietly.

"*Aurat ko hi chup rehna padhta hai. Aadmi jaat aisi hi hoti hai* (Men are the way they are. Women have to keep quiet)," they told me.

Anger, silence, negligent behaviour, patch-ups, hosting or attending a party and then cooling off - the duration of the cycle had reduced and the distance between us was already increasing.

My diary had become my best friend. I would talk to it, share my secrets, take out my frustrations, get angry and sometimes, even cry while penning my feelings down. Probably that is why nobody ever came to know the truth, the ugly façade of my much-admired marriage.

I was living in parallel realities; one was my truth and the other a projection.

> *Dear Diary,*
>
> *I want to break free and run away. I just want to vanish one day from this scene. I want to live freely and happily. I want to feel like I felt with Shiv.*
>
> *- Seeking*
> *Tara*

My pen paused at the last sentence and I immediately cut it.

Where was Shiv? My mind wandered but I quickly discarded the thought and busied myself with something else.

Pritam had also started travelling frequently to avoid the cacophony at home. He would just pack his things and go off alone or with friends. I had started longing for his absence as the interference, manipulation and lies were lesser when he was away. In fact, there was indifference and no communication. I was still worried about Pritam and his obsession for speed. I would pray till he reached his destination. I did not know why I still worried about him, knowing fully well that there was nothing between us. Maybe having nothing held its own space, connecting us in that no-thingness.

Expression of love may be different for everyone but the feeling of being loved is the same.

What comes, goes,
What remains…IS.

Living for each day as it unfolded became routine for me, in thought and in action. I would often pretend to be busy, talk on the phone, laugh and pause at the perfect time. I had created an imaginary world for myself. I realised that grace lay in letting time pass, in not demeaning the partner, especially the one I had loved deeply.

Just because something good or bad happened in the past, it need not remain the same in the present or the future. It is our attachment to the memory which makes us a slave to that emotion. It may give us a feeling of safety but one has to remember that change is the only consistent factor in life. Everything remains in a state of flux, moments, date, time and frequency. In the Universe, every planet, star and even light keeps moving. With the movement in space, there is a change in the vibration, frequency and degree. Perception changes with the shift in reception of the signal. Existence is transient in that moment. The underlying truth is that the Divine All encompasses everything to remain as it is with the movement of change happening, creating and destroying everything within the ALL.

The moment we realise the game of change, the game changes.

One day, I found a set of playing cards that Baba had given me before marriage. I had forgotten how dear they used to be until I saw them again. They were developed by Pt. Madan Gopal who culled the teachings of the *Bhagavad Gita* through them.

The cards have four suits, each representing the different *lokas*. Each card contains virtues associated with that *loka*. Just like the different omens, as soon as I saw the cards again, I asked a question and the cards guided me.

1. ***Swarg Loka*** represents the world of supreme delight. The cards in this suit include purity, *dharma*, vow, mercy, service, charity, *yajna*, penance, truth, *Deva's* messenger, *Devshakti* and *Devraja*.

2. ***Narak Loka*** is where sinners are punished. Greed, fraud, conceit, lust, anger, delusion, *himsa*, ungratefulness, falsehood, *Yama's* messenger, *Yama Shakti and Yama Raja*.

3. ***Karma Loka*** is the world of action. It contains caution, health, education, good conduct, cooperation, patience, effort, faith, prosperity, *Raja's* messenger, *Raja Shakti* and the *Raja*.

4. ***Moksha Loka*** is where eternal peace is attained. These include living alone, self-restraint, detachment, endurance, equality, renunciation, forgiveness, devotion, divine knowledge, Krishna's messenger,

Krishna *Shakti* and Krishna Consciousness.

5.   **Joker**: *Jo-kar,* so *bhar* (As you sow, so shall you reap).

Wanting to get out of the city, someone recommended visiting a palace that had been turned into a hotel. It looked beautiful and majestic in pictures and so a trip was planned with a friend, Rhea. We checked into the hotel and true to its heritage, it was grand.

The room had a heavy antique door with big circular handles made of brass, like a bangle, which we often see on-screen. That night, I heard a knock on the door. I woke up, unsure whether I heard a knock or a sound from outside. I looked around and just as I was going to go back to sleep, there was another knock.

"Who is it?" I called while quickly shaking Rhea awake.

"What happened?" she asked.

"Someone is knocking the door. I asked, but no one replied."

Just then there was another knock.

"See!" I said, pointing to the door.

Rhea looked at me as if I had lost my mind. "Tara, there was no knock. Were you dreaming?" she shook me as if to check if I was awake or not. I glared at her and brushed her hand away from my shoulder, and looked at the door again.

"It is 2:23 A.M. Let us please just go to sleep. And do not open the door to go looking around for the knocker. You must have heard something else and got confused," Rhea said as she plopped back on her bed.

Confused, I went back to sleep. The next morning, we woke up early to go for a walk around the beautiful property before breakfast. We had taken only ten steps into the lawn when I felt my feet and body become heavy. It felt as if someone was pulling me back with great strength, making it difficult for me to walk. About to panic, wondering if it was some medical emergency, I suddenly felt something was wrong.

On a hunch, I asked Rhea to close her eyes and when she opened them, to look straight into mine and without thinking, say the first thing she saw. Surprised, she closed her eyes and as soon as she opened them, she looked into mine and immediately took two steps back, surprised and scared.

"I see a young man," she said.

I comforted her and asked her to carry on while I went back to the room. I lit a candle, prayed and requested the spirit to feel safe to make its presence felt. The spirit appeared. It felt like a young man with a turban and dark circles under his eyes. I bowed, acknowledging his presence, and asked him what he wanted. He said that he had lived in the palace and now wanted to cross over from the mortal world towards the Light.

I asked him to share something as proof of his story. There was no reason or significance behind my asking. I just asked. He shared that the palace had a *tehkhana*, a cellar, with a painting of three tigers behind a glass wall. I performed the rites and freed him.

I joined my friend for breakfast. The manager came around to enquire about our stay and after a brief interaction, I asked if there was a cellar in the palace. He was surprised how I knew about it. I requested if I could visit it once. He went to ask for permission and after ten minutes he returned with a positive reply and brought a bunch of old keys. He led the way across a big, green field and from nowhere a staircase appeared, leading down to a cellar. It was almost like a scene out of a historic movie. As the Manager opened the lock on a wooden door, a dim light lit the corridor. The smell conveyed that the place had not been opened in a long time. In one room, I could see the legs of furniture, peeking out from under sheets that covered it. Another room was full of big carved boxes, antiques and lamps.

"All these things must be carrying so many secrets under all that dust," I thought.

As we continued down the corridor, I almost forgot the purpose of this visit to the cellar until I saw a huge glass partition and froze. Behind it was the painting of the tigers. Young, handsome and beautiful, the three creatures stood tall. Amazed at the sight, I quietly bowed to the departed soul who had approached me.

The next day, as we reached the reception to check out, I casually glanced upwards and saw a painting of a young man in a turban with dark circles under his eyes.

"Who is this young man?" I asked the receptionist.

"This is a painting of a prince of the royal family who own

this palace. I have heard that he died when he was thirty-five years old and was quite fond of hunting," he replied with a smile and handed me the payment receipt.

"There is nothing like darkness. Only the absence of light."
- Jess Bowen

I had been trying to mend my marriage from all quarters of life, through counselling, courses, healing and travelling. In the beginning both of us had fought for our freedom against Veena's hatred, and then it became an individual fight as Pritam struggled with his feelings and I with mine. I fought for my rights and now the fights had become a basic need for survival. There was no reason, love or respect left in the relationship. Both of us were trying to escape a breakdown.

I was beginning to accept that I was scared to move out of this marriage which was becoming poisonous for Pritam and myself. Both of us were in denial of this situation.

At parties and social gatherings, jokes on marriages and affairs were frequent. I would laugh and say, "It is okay. Wherever Pritam goes, at least he returns to me at night," and everyone would laugh out loud. Their laughter kept their partner's secrets safe, concealing their realities.

Even though I was a part of these conversations, I never understood how the sanctity of marriage could easily be mused at and taken for granted. Maa and Baba would never have dared to do something like this and I would make sure my children did not, either.

Good humour is where everyone laughs and enjoys without demeaning anyone. The art of wit and humour can be inherited and also be cultivated into a skill.

I also realised that it is difficult for a man to move out of a loveless marriage than it is for a woman. The moment the latter realises that the marriage is over, she is ready to move out.

Women have always been stronger. They have the liberty to choose who would be theirs and whose baby they want as they are the divine receivers and givers. Mother Earth remains a powerful empowered reality. They hold the strength, depth and desire to flourish, create, hold the creation and protect it. Men may travel to places to earn but they return to one centre, the home, a place where they can rest and recuperate.

I could not understand why Pritam did not just accept his love for Radhika so that we could move on accordingly and respectfully. Every time I asked him, he would either get angry or try to get intimate with me as a consolation. He could not decide what he wanted in life and because of his indecisiveness, he was not only ruining his, mine and Radhika's life but also the children's.

People will bring you down when you are above them.

One day while walking in a busy market, I crossed a full-length mirror. It took me a few minutes to realise what I saw. I retreated my steps and found myself in front of the mirror again, looking at my own reflection. I was unable to recognise myself. Dark circles had appeared under my eyes and I had lost so much weight that I looked frail. That evening, I stood in front of the mirror again, at home. It had been ages since I saw myself. It seemed as if a stranger was standing there.

"Who are you?" I asked.

The reflection replied with the same question, "Who are you?"

"Tara. I am Tara," I replied.

"Not the Tara I know," said the reflection. "You are not what you were named for. You were the light, beaming with joy, laughter and happiness. You are not yourself anymore or what you were meant to be. You were a born a warrior, a *yogini*. You were beautiful and confident, a woman of pride. Look at yourself now, brooding and unhappy. You are wasting yourself and your time."

Tears rolled down my cheeks. I could not look into my eyes

in the mirror anymore.

Days passed and I still could not get myself to face the mirror.

About three weeks later, I was sitting in a restaurant and a smartly dressed Dutch woman came up to me and asked if I was a Shaman.

"Oh no! My name is Tara," I replied with a smile.

I had never heard of the name "Shaman" before. "What an interesting name," I thought to myself when the lady laughed and said, "I did not mean your name, my child. A Shaman is a healer. It is a title that is given. I have been practising for many years and I felt that you are also one."

The tall, beautiful, grey-haired woman simply smiled and left. My eyes followed her graceful gait as she walked out of the restaurant. I thought of searching what a Shaman was, but forgot to do so by the time I got home. A few days later, I encountered this word again. I was invited for dinner where a guest, who had been studying healing modalities and texts at Auroville in Pondicherry, asked me if I was a Shaman. This caught my attention.

I researched, found out and within a week, met a Shaman and got introduced to this healing technique called Shamanism. I learnt that a Shaman is a person who can journey to the altered state of consciousness. They are native healers who align with the power of the ALL, to enter an alternate reality, seeing with closed eyes to receive answers and healings. According to Shamanism, there are three Worlds, the Upper World where angels, spirits and masters reside, the Lower World where animals and plants are present and the Middle World where we exist. Everything present in the Upper and Lower World is also present in the Middle World but humans are not present in the former two Worlds. Shamanism also believes that the cause of any ailment first occurs at the soul level then mental, followed by emotional and lastly affects the physical reality.

A month later, I went to a new country to learn and empower myself. I travelled across time and space where I saw, felt and listened. It made me question who I was and what I was meant to be. Fear and doubt had made its house within me. As I delved into Shamanism, I began to shake off the rust of others' perceptions and judgements of who I was. Just as the priest had told me to "shine like the star that you are, strong and glowing," I could feel something happening. The work had begun!

Each experience made me feel all those emotions again which had exhausted and dried up. I felt like a rock embedded with various jewels. With every effort and travel, the dirt was scraped off each jewel till it shone out bright, and then another was cleansed. Many had been cleaned and uncovered yet many remained. Similarly, aspects of my true being were starting to appear and shine from here and there just like my name, I presume. These travels and teachings eroded what was not required inside me. I was finding myself again. It was not an overnight realisation.

It took me months to first let go of the fears and doubts and then connect with the One to regain what I had lost. It was a constant, conscious effort to keep reminding myself. It was not magic, but it truly was magical for it brought out emotions that I had buried deep within, not realising that trash is always supposed to be thrown out. Hiding it under the bed will only result in its rotting and stinking.

I had the first session for two hours with middle-aged Mexican Shaman. After the session finished, she asked, "Why are you such a perfectionist?"

"Me? No, no, my husband and his mother are perfectionists. I am not even close to being one," I corrected her, sure that she had read me incorrectly.

"I am talking about you, my child. There is a streak of perfectionism and idealism within you. You are looking for a perfect and ideal partnership in this relationship which is difficult and that is why you are suffering."

"You are not happy. You may never have this ideal relationship with this man as there is a different learning for both in this equation," she said.

I was not too pleased with this last line. However, it was too soon for me to realise that the Shaman only told me what she saw. It was not her interpretation and neither did she sugar-coat her words. She delivered the message that she saw in her vision as Shamans do.

I bowed, received her blessings and left.

Shamans see with closed eyes. They journey to parallel realities to get strength, receive blessings and seek information. They always work in partnership with spirits to heal souls, people and the environment to create harmony and balance.

"The Fire is real,
Your fear is not."
- Connie Phelan

The next milestone in Shamanism was the fire walk and for me, it was one of the biggest challenges. When I was six years old, a big bowl of hot curry spilled on my chest leaving me bedridden for almost a month till the burns healed. Since then, I had been frightened of fire or anything hot. My fear had only increased with time, so much so that I would always cool my food and beverage before consuming it. I stayed away from heaters or other appliances associated with heat.

I had heard about Muslim devotees gathering in Lucknow for the 'walk on fire' ritual ahead of Muharram. I had also heard about *sadhus* lying on fire during the Kumbh Mela. Various explanations were offered for this ritual, one of which was that a person accused of a crime or of uttering a lie may be asked to undergo the ordeal of fire to prove his or her innocence, also called the *Agni Pariksha*. If they emerge unscathed, their innocence is proved.

Firewalkers believe that only those who lack faith suffer injuries from the fire, while the faithful are spared. Devotees also undertake firewalking to fulfil their vows.

It was time for me to test myself, to find out if I was ready to take the leap. I did not know what I was doing yet I felt that this walk might give me the courage to cross over my fears.

As the day came closer, I became nervous and anxious. I wondered why I even thought of going through fire, the thing I feared the most.

On the day of the fire walk, the sound of drums, rattlers and *mantras* started, echoing all around as I got ready. The smoke from the *loban* filled the air and the instructor spoke, "We are made of five elements and fire, one of the elements, is what keeps us alive. The Sun is fire and fire is life. It is action. Prepare yourself with the thought that you know how to walk through the fire and you will be able to cross it unhurt and safely."

"The rules are simple. Know that you are one with the element and made of fire. Be the Light, feel it inside you and be confident. Drop all your fears, fill your mind with positive thoughts and be sure that you will simply glide through the burning coals. Do not speed up. Be mindful, firm and keep going. Be the Light and be light on your feet." This last line kept echoing in my mind as I took a deep breath and put my right foot forward.

Watchful, that I have no thoughts going on in my head and in my mindful state, I walked. Lightly, firmly, steadily and consistently, I finished the fifteen feet long stretch of fire.

"That's it? I finished? I crossed the fire? I did it!"

I could not believe it. I had walked on fire and was on the other side, safe and sound. Amidst the sound of the loud drums, I started crying. I had done it. That night I slept as I would after a long journey.

The next day, everyone talked about their experience. No longer afraid, I shared excitedly with the group, "I panic when I see fire as I got burnt when I was a child. Since then, I had been afraid of anything hot, even hot food or water. Standing there last night, I was thinking of running away. I asked myself why do I need to be there? What do I need to prove? The questions came and went, the fear came and went and then something told me to walk on the fire. It was as if I was in a trance. When I did it, I felt that the fire burnt what was not required in my body, mind and soul. I feel I am ready now to take the next step, the next leap. Thank you." I bowed and thanked the instructor for the experience.

I realised then that this was probably why the Tara in me never stood against the emotional and mental turmoil. The fear of getting burnt or hurt kept me away from taking a leap towards joyful and respectful living.

"Water is one of the most important elements on Earth. Our body consists of seventy percent water. Our emotions are stored in water in our cellular memory and we need to recycle it regularly so that we feel fresh and healthy," I listened intently as the teacher, Ida Ayu, spoke about the next experience.

"I will pour water on your head, and you have to stomp your feet and shout as loud as you can. This will help you to open up. Cry if you need to. Keep stomping your feet. Scream and let out all your pent-up emotions."

That year I had gone to Indonesia to further my learning of Shamanism where I met the High Priestess, Ida Ayu, an incarnation of Goddess Kuan Yin, who performed the water ceremony to cleanse everybody of their spiritual and emotional baggage.

"Tara," they announced. I went forward to join the queue, all of us dressed up in sarongs.

I stood in front of the healer chanting *mantras* and a rhythmic, soulful music could be heard in the background.

As soon as I was ready, buckets of chilling water were poured on my head. It sent a shiver down my spine. I stomped my feet but could not shout or cry. Sometimes, shock is needed to come alive. I tried hard but no words or sound came out of my mouth. I stomped my feet harder, still I was unable to open my mouth. Tears rolled down my cheeks and yet, I was silent.

After the ceremony, a volunteer called me inside the temple where the Priestess was sitting. She was beautiful. In her pristine dress and flowers in her hair, she looked divine.

"You seem to have locked up too many emotions. If you do not resolve them, you might fall prey to illness and depression. Talk to someone. Open up and tell your truth. Be authentic to yourself. Know that you are the blessed one. Be kind to yourself. If you will not let go of your fears and pent-up emotions, you will cease to exist. You will live like the dead. Be bold and courageous. Do justice to yourself. If not for yourself, then for whom? If not now, then when?" she said.

I raised my head to look at the Priestess, I could only see her glow. I heard a prayer with a bell and smelt *loban*.

She continued, "So I ask you, Tara. Are you ready to take the leap? Remember, once you are ready, the soul will know. Then the whole Universe will conspire to make your wants come true. Listen to your soul and tell me if you are ready, Tara. Remember, being a Warrior-*Yogini*, it is your duty to save yourself before you inspire other souls to reach their goals and their soul's desires. This is your last birth and it is important to complete the transactions. Yet, along with completing the transactions, it is your responsibility to transform and the moment you let go of the desire to hold on, the transition to the next realm will arrive swiftly and smoothly."

Sounds of bells, drums and chants surrounded me. With folded hands I said, "Yes, I am ready to live a respectful life. A life with trust, joy and peace. Thank you, thank you, thank you." The Priestess hugged me and gifted me a white feather. I bowed and left the space feeling still in trance.

As I walked on the gravelled path, I stopped suddenly and looked back at the temple in astonishment and in gratitude, recalling the Priestess' words, "Warrior-*Yogini*". How did she know about my conversation with the reflection in the mirror? Amazed, I smiled thinking about the mysterious ways in which the Universe works. Power and insight that great souls have is often beyond imagination and comprehension. It is here that miracles occur.

Sometimes not finding the right words to describe the feelings, conveys it right…

On my return, I had a layover in Kuala Lumpur. Having stopped there once before, I had come across a Malaysian chocolate that I absolutely loved. This time, I had already thought of buying a few extra ones to bring back home. As I got off the plane and entered the airport, I asked around and found the café where I had tried the chocolate earlier.

It was early morning, and I ordered a cup of coffee and the chocolate I loved. However, they informed me that the stock would reach after an hour. Disappointed, as I had to board the plane in forty minutes, I requested the lady at the counter to check once in case they had it.

With few customers at that hour, the lady stood on her toes and searched the cupboard, that was at a height, but could not find it. She apologised and offered me other chocolates to buy instead. Declining with a smile, I thanked her and continued with the white coffee. As I had my last sip of that great coffee, a speciality of Malaysia, I requested the lady if she could check one last time.

The lady felt bad for me but also let out a little laugh at the pout I had on my face unknowingly. It reminded her of a small child asking for candy. Unable to resist that face, she invited me to look in the cupboard myself. With a big smile

I quickly made my way to the cupboard. Thanking her, I stretched my hand in search of the chocolate.

I caught hold of something stuck in the corner, grabbed it and as I lowered my arm, I almost jumped with amazement when I saw the same brand that I wanted. Maybe it was a mirage, like the illusion of water in a desert. The lady's gasp brought me back to reality and confirmed that it was the same chocolate and not a trick of my mind. Standing behind me, she was quite surprised since she had already checked the cupboard twice.

Sometimes, it is the little joys that make a day. All the way to the boarding gate, I was smiling to myself and at whoever looked at me. As I made myself comfortable on a seat, I decided to have the chocolate while I waited for the boarding announcement.

I pulled the bar out and noticed its date of manufacture. It was my birth date and month. It was insane! I laughed to myself.

I did not realise who I was until I stopped being who I was not.

I was still sleeping when Veena's loud voice woke me up. "What does she do? She goes abroad, comes back and sleeps till late. Is she a queen? She does nothing as she does not know anything. It is only the servants who are managing the house. What are these spiritual workshops? Such a waste of time and money. If she is so religious, she should attend the *satsang* at Mrs. Bhatia's house with me. Why does she not pray every morning? Good, religious daughters-in-law go to the temple on Tuesdays and keep a fast every Monday and Friday. Why does she not do that? She just knows how to waste money."

I heard every word Veena said, got up and went for a bath. I was surprised that this time I did not cry under the shower. I took my bath, longer than usual, stood in front of the mirror, massaged my body with firm movements, dressed up, entered the kitchen, wished Veena, told the cook to make my tea and went to the terrace to savour it peacefully.

I was not sure if it had stopped affecting me because I had accepted this behaviour as an ultimate reality or I had become strong enough to not let it disturb me anymore.

"Why are you in this relationship?" Farida asked me.

I repeated the question. The question I asked myself ever so frequently without clarity, reason or any semblance of an answer. I had only excuses to offer till now.

Looking at my hands, resting on my lap, I did not know how to respond or chose not to since my return from Indonesia as I was in 'the silence stage'. I did not want to talk to anyone or give any answers. I just wanted peace. I knew that Pritam had agreed for his parents to shift in because it was easier for him to keep me embroiled in their petty games.

"Do you know this is an abusive relationship?" Farida continued firmly this time.

I had once used this word in front of Pritam and he had become quite angry. "Abusive? Do you even know what it means? What is abusive about our relationship? You are given money to spend, you can buy jewellery, visit places and have big cars to flaunt. It is because of my status and circle that you have an amazing social life. I have given you everything, much more than you can imagine or deserve. What if I have broken a few things? TVs, phones, plates, glasses can be purchased again. Imagine if I had not done that then you could have been hit. So, zip your lips and stop complaining. There is no need to be an idealist. All marriages have faults, dents and bruises. You should be grateful to me for without me, you are nothing."

"Tara, if you had to describe Pritam in five sentences, what would you say?" Farida's voice brought me back to reality.

I looked at her blankly.

"Quick. Do not think. Describe Pritam to me," she reiterated.

"He is extremely hard working," I said. "But he is selfish and shrewd like no other that I have seen."

"He is helpful when he wants to be. I feel that he is helpful when it is useful for him. He will keep a count of it and cash in on that favour when he needs it."

"He displays himself to be so many things that are textbook appropriate or beneficial for himself or his ego - loving, generous, humble, polite and well-mannered. In reality, he has no emotions. He can be ruthless and merciless."

"He wears many masks and changes them swiftly."

"He is very conscious of his personal and public image. What people think of him is very important for him."

"Oh shit," Farida exclaimed. "How did I not see this earlier," she gasped.

I wondered if I had said anything wrong. "What happened?" I asked her.

"Tara, I think you are living with a narcissist!" she said. "I cannot say for certain without having met him and doing a proper analysis but these are classic traits of a narcissist. I wonder how I missed it for so long."

Four days later Farida met Pritam which confirmed her suspicions. Soon after, I had an email waiting for me in my inbox.

<u>Characteristics and red flags to look out for in people with Narcissism:</u>

- ❖ Grandiosity: These people have an exaggerated sense of self-importance. They have a constant need to feel superior to others and get special treatment. Their irrational feeling of having a larger-than-life image is often accompanied by fantasies of unlimited success, brilliance, power, beauty and love.

- ❖ Excessive need for admiration: They feel mistreated, depleted and enraged when ignored. They have a need to be the centre of attention. Their best weapon is to ignore others when disagreed with.

- ❖ Superficial and exploitative relationships: For them relationships are a means to reach somewhere and not a bond to feel and rejoice. They will be with you till your presence is beneficial for them. They often find a partner who is an empath.

- ❖ Lack of empathy: They are devoid of emotions. They lack the ability to care about the emotional needs or experiences of others. Even their closest ones feel neglected and objectified. They do not express or understand emotions as emotions rather as objects to be either kept or thrown away.

❖ Identity disturbance: Their sense of self is highly superficial, rigid and fragile. Even small ups and downs have more impact on their identity than is required. They are scared and lonely at heart.

❖ Chronic feelings of emptiness and boredom: When attention and praise is not available, these people feel empty, bored, depressed and restless. They want people to keep praising their smallest efforts in a grand way and should sing their praises every now and then. They are swift liars.

❖ Manipulative: They know how to manipulate and make you question your reality. They create a façade of a perfect life and family. However, in reality they are weak and their relations are distorted and dysfunctional. They demand prime importance at every moment in your life, so much so that your entire life starts to revolve around them, and their needs and aspirations.

Narcissists try to destroy your life with lies,
Because theirs can be destroyed with the truth.

Stay with the ones who loved you as a whole when you thought you were in pieces.

I still remember the day Pritam and I had bought our first two-wheeler. We had been saving up money and planning for months. It was our first big purchase together. We were too excited. For the first few months, we would go out for a ride almost every evening, sometimes, even late at night. I would sit behind Pritam with my arms around his waist and my head resting against his back. Soon, he taught me how to drive.

Eventually, we had to toss a coin as to who would drive first. It was not as much about the driving but about being together and having fun. Every weekend, we would go out for our favourite street food *bhelpuri* and *chole bhature*, or friends would come over to our house and we would dance and sing until the wee hours of the morning. Since we were the first ones to have our own space, our house became the "hangout spot".

Everyone came to our house for different reasons, some found solace, some came to party and others to just be themselves. It was a home we built with love and honesty. Pritam and I never bought a bed and instead purchased five mattresses for we always had guests and friends over, and we loved it. Whenever we were alone, Pritam would cuddle me and we would sleep entangled with each other as one. There was an enviable harmony between us.

How did we go from being that to this? A narcissist and an empath? I wondered sometimes if I was living in an illusion. I did not know how life slipped from my hands. Was he always like that? How did I miss the pattern?

"Maybe I could fix this relation with more time, effort and love. Now that I know that he has a personality disorder, I am sure we can work on it and fix our relationship. Everything can be mended with extra understanding and love. He probably needs me the most right now," I said to myself.

"If you love a person, give them infinite space." - Osho
If you want to destroy a person, take away their space.

It is said if you want to break someone, break his or her belief system. Break the conditioning of the mind to change the story. Pritam started telling me that I was required at the office for important projects and I needed to keep my work on a backburner. The moment I would do that, I was asked to prioritise the house. When I would focus on the house, he would make me sit and tell me sweetly, "You are doing so well in your work, you should concentrate on that. We can handle office work. For the house, hire more people. Do not let these things affect your work." Then suddenly, he would cancel all my meetings and sessions, and make me attend to some "urgent office work".

It was frustrating for I was trying to focus on everything and unable to finish anything. I constantly felt like a failure who could not manage my work or things at home, along with official commitments. Was I really as useless as Veena and Pritam always claimed? I did not know then that it was just a game for Pritam to make me feel incompetent. I was so caught up in his game that weaved around me like a spider's web, entangling me every single day.

His manipulations were coupled with constant reinforcements that I was good for nothing.

"There is no contribution of yours in my life anymore," he would say every now and then.

"You misbehave with my parents. Behave the way I want you to otherwise you will have nowhere to go."

"Do not dare to interfere in Radhika's work. She is looking after everything in the office."

"You should be thankful to me, my parents and Radhika."

"Are you really this stupid or do you do it to annoy me?"

My belief about myself had started changing. Maybe I was "good for nothing".

Despite everything, I ensured that our external reality remained unfazed. People considered us to be an ideal couple - confident, successful and much in love. Nobody knew the truth. As if anybody cared, I thought.

Pritam would often say that friends come for parties and nothing more. I realised that he was right. No one cared what happened before and after the party.

"Radhika is getting a divorce," Pritam announced one morning.

Radhika had become such an integral part of our life that anything that happened in her life affected ours.

I saw the warning in his eyes, that I should neither interfere nor object. The concern in his voice for Radhika and the love he felt for her used to upset me a lot. That day, it did not. I had begun to respect Radhika, the woman my husband had chosen. She was his confidante and lover now.

People easily blamed the other person for destroying a marriage. I believed that a relationship was already broken, if there was space for another person to enter. Only Pritam and I were to be blamed for the state of our relationship. Others were just catalysts to increase the distance between us.

I also knew that if I even suggest that we separate, he would ruin my life. I used to fear him and his actions but now fear was fading away gradually, as my life was already a living hell.

I could see that he was becoming like his mother, a compulsive liar.

Love coupled with trust is the most beautiful emotion to hold onto in life. I was starting to accept that he had fallen out of love with me, and so had I. What upset me was his behaviour towards me. It was difficult to decide if his words hurt more or his actions. "Do I really want this man or this marriage?" I asked myself and pat came the reply, "No".

"Does Pritam want me or this marriage?" I asked again and the reply was, "No".

As clarity within me improved, so did time. Days suddenly flew at double the speed. It is said that when the destination is close, the speed increases.

Amidst the chaos at home, the silence within grounded me. I chose to become soul deaf. I was busy working on myself, speeding up the process, with the understanding that there was a master plan for each one of us and there was a free will which prevailed as well.

I felt that I just had to tell the Universe what I truly wanted and soon that time would come.

On a beautiful *Basant* morning, I sat in silence on my terrace and prayed to the Supreme All for someone who had similar desires with the same intensity to give and receive love. The soul who mirrored my longing to have a simple, transparent, respectful and joyful relationship with the partner, and together we would experience a healthy, happy and fulfilling connection.

Two frogs fell into a deep pit while travelling through the woods. Other frogs kept shouting in despair and helplessness. One frog lost his life hearing the discouragement. The other tried harder and leapt out of the pit and survived. He was a deaf frog.

When I had learnt Angel Therapy, a few attendees shared their experiences of hosting angels or visiting houses of acquaintances where angels had visited. Since then, I also wished for the same and asked my teacher how I could host them. I was told that when the time was right, angels would come calling on their own. Since then, I waited patiently for my turn.

After a few months, I started receiving signs. From picking up a book on angels to receiving an old coin from my aunt, I knew in my heart that this was not a coincidence. One glorious morning while walking in Lodhi Gardens, I saw a feather and stopped to pick it up, then another and then a bunch of them. That day, I received a message from a friend that angels were at her house and enquired if I would be interested to welcome them for three days.

"Yes," I almost shouted in excitement filled with gratitude and happiness.

I was told that angels made their presence felt and it was not possible to see them with naked eyes. However, I could keep a camera on and would be able to see orbs on it. Confused and excited, I did as others guided. On the night when the angels were supposed to arrive, I had a special altar prepared for them which was well-lit with candles, white flowers, feathers and toffees.

I was present at the doorstep with a candle in my hands and camera on the side. As if on cue, I suddenly saw multiple orbs of light on the camera screen, entering my house. The moment I looked away from the camera, I spotted nothing in the darkness. The picture on the camera screen looked exactly like pictures of clustered stars I had seen in books. The light reminded me of my name. "I am Tara. I welcome you to my home to bless us and to be with us. Thank you," I said the prayer and welcomed the angels in.

For the next three days, word spread that angels were visiting my house. Soft and soulful angelic music was played throughout their stay. Guests were welcome to come, sit in silence or pray to the angels. I kept flowers and sweets which could be offered to the angels.

On the last evening of their stay, I was surprised to see so many people, known and unknown, visit my house to meditate together. For an hour, there was complete silence and each person experienced the quietness differently and individually. It was a beautiful yet humbling experience. That night, I thanked the angels and requested them to visit a friend's house. I saw on the camera screen as the orbs of light drifted into the night sky.

The next day, an acquaintance, unaware of the angels' visit, called me to share that she was crossing my house the previous evening and felt a huge aura around the house. She had stopped the car, awestruck to witness such grandeur.

It was a breathtaking event.

*"Cherish those who seek the truth
But beware of those who find it."*
- Voltaire

The beauty of Shamanism for me was the direct connection with the worlds to receive strength, guidance and healing. It does not have any *guru* or holy person who is followed. There are, of course, teachers who share their knowledge and learning but that is it. Their role completes the moment the workshop ends. It is focused on the person and their soul journey. It is a link with the spirits, angels and the ALL. A Shaman always works in partnership with the spirits. It is said that all Shamans are healers but all healers are not Shamans.

It is almost unbelievable and easy to doubt. Can we really travel across time and space? Was it real what I was viewing and experiencing? The instructions were loud and clear, "Be hollow, have clear intent, and trust what you see and hear."

The visions became more intense as I became silent. I had always enjoyed the sounds of silence. In the humdrum of guests and constant flow of visitors, I had found my space and time for silence. In noise, I recognised the frequency of harmony. In the crowd, I had learnt the skill to be connected to my core.

As the degree and frequency of silence increased, I realised it was a familiar feeling linked to my childhood. In that house, I had felt the same solace. I remember vividly how I always had my quiet time - that was mine to cherish, think, introspect and connect. I had lost it over the years, only for it to find me again. Now, I valued it with all my might. I was picking up bits and pieces of my true self that I had either forgotten or left behind.

Between the teachings of my parents, the learning of my soul and the changes I was seeing in my life, I had found a rhythm of flow. During my inward journeys, I could now objectify the subjectivity and vice versa. The balance between strong and strength was beginning to unfold. I could tap into the zone where there was nothing and its presence helped me to live in the present. The challenge was to increase the duration of the zeroness, *shunya*, the silence in my head and heart. As I met new facets of my own being every day, it grounded me to bring equilibrium not only within but also reflect it externally. The silence was different from numbness, a feeling I had become familiar with.

Earlier, with uncontrollable and defeating events, I had to forget and go numb. Now, slowly and steadily I was regaining my strength and courage to make an effort to come alive, yet again. I started viewing situations as an observer. Words like honesty, integrity, authenticity, transparency and acceptance appeared more in my conversations.

The Astral travels had opened many arenas and visions for me. Whenever I sought an answer for myself or others, I would travel across time and space, and return with learning or the reply. Each time, I was awestruck thinking about the magic and its radiance.

I was all set to go to Thailand for a workshop and hotel was booked much in advance. However, when I was checking in, the receptionist at the front desk informed me that there was some problem in the allotted room and because of the inconvenience caused, they would be upgrading me to a suite.

Who does not love a free upgrade to a suite? That too with a private Jacuzzi! Hello, Thailand!

Excited, I thanked the staff and followed the bellboy to the two-storied cottage.

I was thrilled. I unpacked my bags, took a hot shower and was preparing my first cup of coffee when I felt I saw someone coming down the stairs of the suite. I was not sure if I saw someone or felt a presence. I could not differentiate between the two. Just like a handyman always carries his tools, I always carry a tealight with me. I took my coffee to the room, lit a candle and spoke to the Energy.

"Hello, I am Tara. I have come here for a course on alternate realities and the spirit world. I had booked a room in this hotel but there was some problem and they gave me this suite instead. Please allow me to stay here for a fortnight and I ensure I will not disturb you. I hope you will understand and I want to thank you for making your presence felt. I look forward to a peaceful co-existence. I assure you, once again, that I will not intrude into your energy space. Thank you."

The next fifteen days were amazing. I learnt a lot during the course and unlearned even more. It was enlightening and liberating. The Energy and I were living like housemates. It was surprising, on hindsight, that I never felt scared of the presence. In fact, it was oddly comforting. Every evening, as I returned back to the room, I talked to the Energy, sharing stories from the day.

On the last day, I thanked my invisible housemate for letting me stay in her house and for the wonderful time we shared peacefully. Unsure if the experience was true or just my imagination, I felt like the Energy was a friend from a life lived before.

The next year, I revisited Thailand and was booked in a different hotel. Fondly remembering my previous stay, I enquired about that hotel and its distance from the current hotel while I was checking in. The manager shared that the hotel had been shut down a few months earlier as it was found to be haunted.

As the experiences increased, I realised that they were of no use if I did not change my outlook or course of action. What then, was the use of gaining all this knowledge and being blessed by great masters if I was not executing the learning and releasing myself of pain and continuous suffering?

The course of action was not to keep attending courses and workshops, but to act on the learning. I needed to be fearless and calm. To be empowered, one should be able to create a new reality with awareness and conscious efforts, and not carry on in the parallel reality of illusions. It was important to accept the state of being in the moment, the reality of my relationship with myself in this marriage.

One of my healer friends made me realise that I was playing the victim card as Farida had mentioned earlier. How was I not taking any action to live fully and completely? Was I fearful somewhere deep inside or hopeful that the situation may improve? As I assessed my external situation and internal feelings, I comprehended that I was ready to bring a change and in this new knowledge, I gradually stopped feeling guilty and stopped crying.

Just as for a healthy relationship both the partners have to play their parts and maintain a balance, similarly within us lies the yin and yang. Their roles are defined, often as a masculine and feminine energy that needs to complement each other for a harmonious existence. Likewise, the blessing of *Sukh* and *Shanti* is granted together. *Sukh* represents the external material gains and worldly possessions while *Shanti* is internal peace. The beauty is that no matter which concept or philosophy you follow, this duality resides within each of us and a balance between the two forms the ultimate union of energies.

There is creation, preservation and death in every moment. Brahma, Vishnu and Mahesh are present at that moment. I felt there is a need to live with the essence of the trinity.

"A man of knowledge lives by acting, not by thinking about acting. The trick is in what one emphasises. We either make ourselves miserable or we make ourselves happy. The amount of work is the same. All paths are the same, leading nowhere. Therefore, pick a path with a heart!" - Carlos Castaneda

One evening, just before dinner, I was folding clothes and making a pile of Pritam's clothes and a separate one of mine to be put in the closet. Little did I know that the pile of clothes was not the only separation happening. Pritam entered the room and announced that for 40 days he would practice *brahmacharya*.

Within an hour, bedrooms were separated, his clothes and things were moved to a different room and he stopped talking to me. I noticed that the silence and distance was only reserved for me and gradually, others realised it too. It seemed that a soap opera was being played out at home.

I had stopped letting his actions affect me but no matter how many workshops you attended and great masters you listened to, when such things happened, it hurt somewhere deep down. We had been married for so long. What a waste of a life, I confirmed the thought. I was tired of his manipulations and mind games. I felt like a character in a video game who kept battling one obstacle after the other. I was mentally and emotionally exhausted, trying to maintain my peace and sanity.

On the 32nd day of Pritam's "*brahmacharya*", he entered my bedroom, had sex and announced that forty days had started afresh.

"Kehte hain log ki hum khush mijazi hain

Hum bhi bol pade,
Yeh toh upar wale ki mehr hai, dost
Warna kiski rooh nahi kaampi aur aansu jholi mein na aye."

(People say that I am a happy soul. "This is a blessing
of God, otherwise no one is spared from bad times and
everyone gets scared," I replied.)

"Are you mad? Is your life a joke to you? How are you even letting this happen, Tara?" Farida asked.

"Do you realise that this is a toxic relationship? Have you ever heard of this term? Do you even realise what you are doing to yourself?"

"Look at me, Tara," she almost shouted. "Are you sure you understand what they teach you at your spiritual workshops? Are you still hopeful, confused, scared or do you enjoy being a victim and feeling pity? If not for your sake, please, at least clarify for mine. It seems you have money and do not mind spending it on counselling and healing workshops. Maybe you are just too scared to act and bring about a change.

Tara, either stop coming here and venting out your feelings, or if you are truly hurt, then create boundaries and have the courage to walk out of this abusive marriage. Narcissists are so full of fear that they induce fear in others by their threatening words and actions. Remember, when you create your boundaries, others will know theirs.

I am starting to wonder if you even listen to what I say or come here just to pass time. What do you want to prove to yourself? That you are a martyr, idealist, escapist, coward or a changemaker?"

As Farida kept talking, anger was evident in her words and

tone. I listened silently. Farida was right but I also knew that the drama had begun and this was just the stage setting. Things were going to change soon. A storm was brewing and I could feel the winds.

On the way back home, I followed the Green Light Rule. Thoughts streamed and I let them flow.

"Discipline, as understood by a warrior, is creative, open, and produces freedom. It is the ability to face the unknown, transforming the feeling of knowing into reverent astonishment; of considering things that exceed the scope of our habits, and daring to face the only war that is worthwhile: The battle for awareness."
- Carlos Castaneda

Ping! My phone displayed the notification of a new email in my inbox. "Toxic relationships," the subject line said. Farida had sent an email about what she had talked about in the last session.

Toxic Relationships

According to the Merriam-Webster Dictionary, 'toxic' is defined as, "containing or being poisonous material especially when capable of causing death."

What is a Toxic Relationship?

Simply put, when a relationship becomes shameful, with signs of mental, physical or emotional abuse, it is termed a toxic relationship for there is more disrespect and manipulation rather than support and harmony.

Who are Toxic People?

Toxic people are like the red lights of life, an indication for us to stop and reflect on our emotional, physical, social and psychological investment in a person or a relationship. They can be a boss, partner, friend or a relative who serve as liabilities in the form of their toxicity that leads to a state of physical and mental exhaustion.

Toxic people will drain us of our energy, leading to a burnout. That is when we realise that we need to keep away from such people as they do not contribute to our growth, rather inhibit it in all possible ways.

<u>Signs that a person is Toxic</u>

- ❖ Their actions, words, gestures and conversations are abusive and draining.
- ❖ They belittle you and demean your existence.
- ❖ They slaughter your self-respect and self-worth every time they interact.
- ❖ They make you doubt yourself and forget your strengths.
- ❖ They engage in loud arguments to pull you down.
- ❖ They make you feel angry and resentful.
- ❖ They become stubborn with their personal and professional decisions even if they are not taking the right stand.
- ❖ They enjoy walking over you and disrespecting your boundaries.
- ❖ They disconnect all your well-wishers and make you live an artificial life with them on their terms and conditions.
- ❖ They will question your intelligence and intuition.

Remember: Toxic people are toxic only when you give them your strength. Just like a driver can only drive a car from the driving seat and not from the back seat. Giving them the steering of your life-car is what breaks you and gives them a chance to control you, be harsh and fill you with self-doubts rather than making you feel proud of yourself.

<u>How to move away from such people and their toxicity?</u>

* Identify them and their role in your life.

* Try and avoid physical proximity for they can be verbally or physically abusive.

* Understand their pattern - their behaviour, strengths and weaknesses.

* After you have identified their behavioural and mental loops, draft a mental map tapping your strengths to communicate through it.

* They will try to create an environment of superficial care to cage you in their plans. Draw strong boundaries and take a stand against them.

* Do not let them violate your boundaries for you are no longer a puppet of their toxicity.

* Stay determined to pursue your path even if they emotionally manipulate you.

Remember: Make your bruises your weapons to succeed over their mind games. Nothing is impossible if you have the intent, courage and willpower to choose and create. Life starts afresh at every stage - be it shifting houses or shifting of people in our lives. Ask for help!

When you decide to shift, do not let the fear of the unknown grip you. What is unknown is limited to your mind to scare you, coaxing you to come towards what is familiar. What it does not tell you is that the unknown is just different. Sometimes, you need to shift to that territory because the known is toxic for you and harming you rather than serving or enhancing you.

In such situations, even the unknown is a safer space.

Know yourself - what makes you happy and lets you thrive.

Your life becomes a joke when you make a clown of yourself.

How many of us have cribbed about a poor appraisal or at least heard of friends complaining about it? Almost everyone.

Pritam was sitting across the table from me filling up a self-evaluation form. It was not for the performance of employees at the office rather my "performance and contribution in the house". The evaluation form included pointers such as touching parents' feet every morning, keeping cupboards tidy and cleanliness of the bathroom shower.

Bizarre, right? That was my life. I was living with a narcissist in a toxic relationship. Never in my wildest dreams had I ever envisioned such a future for myself. Despite my recent realisations and awareness, Pritam made sure to keep me entangled with him. I felt like a bee who went in search of a flower and got caught in the Venus flytrap.

I sat there with my mouth firmly shut, listening to Pritam list my mistakes and areas of improvement. It was ironic that the previous evening I came across a new word while reading a magazine sitting in the office reception, 'Gaslighting'.

"Gaslighting is a form of psychological manipulation and mental-emotional abuse. As part of the process, a victim's self-esteem is severely damaged, and one becomes additionally dependent on the gaslighter for emotional support and validation. The phenomenon is attested in the clinical literature as a form of narcissistic abuse. Herein, the gaslighter converts vulnerable people into intellectual and emotional slaves to satisfy their need for constant affirmation and self-esteem," I searched online and read on Britannica's website.

I was handed over the filled form with extensive notes. I was reminded that Pritam was the boss but I was to listen to Veena and DC also as they knew better than us regarding our home and our life.

As I got up to leave Pritam warned, "Think it over Tara, and if you still continue to live the same way and do not mend your ways then you can pack your bags and leave."

I recalled meeting a lady about fifteen years older than me. With a decade more of wisdom, she shared how she had used every aspect of *kootniti* in her marriage - *saam*, *daam*, *dand* and *bhed*. She had lost her husband a few years earlier. He had loved her dearly and she advised everyone to follow her advice, "Marriage is nothing but a trade in India. A woman should believe that she is the Queen and so she should learn all the tricks of the trade. Marriage is a battlefield and each woman should be trained for it."

I tried to bargain and negotiate in this marriage and underwent all the stages of grief - denial, anger, bargaining, depression and finally acceptance. If Pritam behaved well, I did too. If he was silent, I also had nothing much to say. But I could never reason out his misbehaviour. It used to pain me when he attacked my self-esteem, which now I understood was a narcissist's game.

I often remembered Baba's words to marry into a family which had the same character of thought. It was his experience and wisdom that had spoken these words, whose meaning and value I understood now. At that young age, I believed that love could change it all, overcome differences and obstacles. Little did I know that love would change all. Between the 'could' and 'would', love did change and the change, changed all.

Love could conquer all,
Love could transform all,
Yes. Sure. Definitely.
If only, you love at all.

There are three types of relationships between couples: thriving, draining and exhausting. A thriving relationship fulfils the basic requirements and includes all the elements of a trustful rapport. A relationship starts to stray if there is emotional draining. Herein, one can refill it from other sources and still stay in the marriage.

When there is mistrust, lack of respect and communication, abuse, and all resources are over, with both partners having nothing left to offer, the relationship starts eroding, until it exhausts. Our marriage had ended and we had grown apart. We were incompatible, the rest were just excuses and the habit of hanging on.

That evening, I received a five-page long email from him about my incompetence, poor behaviour and how upset he was because of me. It started when he wanted to throw a party for our friends. That evening just before dinner, few of the guests huddled around me curious about my recent spiritual workshop and the experiences I had. The email rambled on about how they were his guests, his friends and so he should have been the centre of attention, "and not you, your trip or your wasteful learning".

It was funny that when arrangements had to be made, food had to be prepared and the house had to be in order to host people, they were "our" guests and I was responsible for everything. If for any reason, I was quiet or had limited interaction with the guests, then I was a "rude host who has spoiled Pritam's image". If I interacted normally, then I was an attention stealer trying to get "overly pally with his guests".

I did not have to read his email to know its contents. I scanned through it, noticing the usual sentences of his kindness towards me; his giving me money, comforts and staff; and his paying my salary in time. There were a few subtle comparisons with Radhika, how Veena was right about me and finally, how I should obey what Pritam, DC and Veena said.

Once, after a night of heavy drinking he told me in one of his neutral moods, "Tara, you know you are like my doll, a toy. I can do anything to you. Dress you up, undress you, hold you tight, lock you in a cupboard but nobody should dare touch you or even look at you. Do you remember what that useless business associate Srinivas had said at the party? That I am a smart and shrewd businessman. If I like someone, I will make them a God and God forbid something goes wrong, I can destroy the person. Remember his words, Tara. If I can make you, I can break you too. You are mine. Never forget that."

I was like a doll, he could cut my hair, twist my arm, attach it again, throw it in a drawer, cling it to his chest or stab me in the heart.

I can never forget that moment when he was reeking of alcohol, eyes red, his hand on my neck and words coming out of his mouth like venom. *"Tu khilona hai mere liye. Jaise jee chahega, waise rakhoonga. Chhodhne ki koshish kari toh dekhna kya karunga* (You are a toy for me. I will treat you the way I want. You cannot even imagine what I will do if you try to leave me)," he said.

Yes, the spiritual learning and journeys had made me strong but nothing prepared me for this. As a child I had learnt the phrase, "sticks and stones may break my bones but words can never hurt me." How wrong that was, I realised. One can still heal from the wounds caused by physical strength but emotional and mental attacks damage us more and affect us deeply.

During the introduction session of a spiritual workshop, the mentor asked everyone what made us attend. When my turn came to answer I shared that I wanted to know why I was with Pritam in this marriage.

I did not have an answer then and I do not have one now.

"Other times, I look at my scars and see something else: a girl who was trying to cope with something horrible that she should never have had to live through at all. My scars show pain and suffering, but they also show my will to survive. They are part of my history that will always be there."
- Scars by Cheryl Rainfield

Dukh ko itni jagah mat do ki dard ban jaye.

"Tara, walk out of this relationship," Farida said.

"You will suffocate and die if you continue this way. Right now, it is as if you have a splinter of wood piercing your skin. Instead of taking it out you are going to the doctor every week and crying but not doing anything about it. Either you take the splinter out or learn to live with the pain. You are wasting my time with your indecision and inaction. Please stop coming to me if you do not want to change your life," Farida spoke in anger and frustration.

"Pritam will keep you busy in the loop of triangulation. You will remain stuck and lose yourself someday."

I knew what Farida meant and where she came from. I did not know how to explain to her that the events were unfolding as per the wishes of the Universe.

For the first time, I felt in control and aligned to my core. There was a strange kind of calmness and stillness in me. I knew I had to decide fast what I wanted. Instead of just living in the present, I had to fix my future too.

Rumi, a Sufi mystic, rightly said, "These pains you feel are messengers. Listen to them" and "You were born with wings, why prefer to crawl through life?"

It is interesting that when you lose interest in something, the attention moves and now my focus had shifted to myself. It was my time to stop crawling and just be with myself. I had to decide when.

I could sense what was going to unfold, the next step and his upcoming behaviour. The yell of the soul was loud, "Walk Out". Somewhere deep down, I was pleased with myself for knowing in advance - a premonition.

Sometimes, God breaks your heart to save your soul.

FREEDOM

"Souls tend to go back to who feels like home." - N.R. Hart

A healer friend told me about the significance of Akashic Records. I looked it up online and was overwhelmed with the information available. So far, I had learnt and worked on different kinds of healing modalities like karmic debts, soul healing, aura cleansing, *chakra* alignment, emotional balancing and energy work. Akashic Records worked on the human consciousness.

I was told that every person has a record that holds personal information about their past, present and possible futures. It is as if every person has their own website on the internet, which they can access anytime. The only difference being that the records are like a living being, forever updating as the person evolves with each thought, feeling and action.

My friend guided me on this journey to view my records

where I understood more than I saw. It was fulfilling to tap into that cosmic world, the journey was smooth and peaceful. I could feel my breath becoming so subtle that at times, I had to check if I was still breathing. There was no boundary of time and space in that realm.

When I accessed my Akashic Records, I reached a place that looked like a library - only that it was huge! It was like a scene out of a science fiction or a fantasy movie where there are millions of books with no end in sight. As I ran my hand along the hardbound books, I caught my name on one of them.

It had a dull golden cover, like a well-aged book. I pulled it out and saw my name, and date and time of birth written on it. As I flipped through the pages I realised that it held my story. Every joy, regret, smile, tear, hurt, surprise, anger, guilt, hope and wish was in this book. It also predicted the date of my arrival to visit and read my records. The future was challenging and it mentioned my soul death. As I read my future, I had a strong urge to rewrite my story on those beige pages that looked similar to the handmade paper I love.

I went to a small, round wooden table with a pen and ink pots. I sat on the chair that was placed next to it, picked up the golden pen and carefully dipped it in the ink pot with red colour and wrote what my heart truly desired.

My thoughts were getting clearer as I wrote in that cosmic world about what I wanted my life to be.

"I am living a respectful, loving and peaceful life with my

partner and children. I am healthy, happy and spiritually aligned. Thank you."

Once I was done, I put the book in a different row, rotated the column, the Light engulfed the library and everything disappeared in a cloud.

What an experience it was! With little knowledge about the outcome, I trusted it as I had learnt to trust myself. It is trust which encourages one to take a leap. I had also learnt about the importance of choices, prioritising and drawing boundaries accompanied with strong will, mindset and a burning desire to keep walking towards the soul goal.

It is said, "The soul deciphers information and transmits it to your heart and mind." I had written my soul's desires.

I respected the supreme plan that is there for each one of us. Yet, I believe that at every turn, there is a choice whether to follow it or change your course. It is this free will which defines our next path. It is similar to the GPS which shows the shortest and fastest route to reach the destination within an expected time. If we try a different route, it reminds us to re-centre and if we continue on our newly chosen path, it will also change its course to accommodate ours.

This is exactly what life does to us.

My attention had shifted, vision cleared and I had asserted my free will to change my reality. I was ready to embrace a new future for myself, on my terms.

Nobody tells you this but sometimes the healing hurts more than the wound.

To clear and cleanse my system internally, I went through each emotion - felt, lived, understood, resolved and rechecked. I picked up threads and shreds, opened the knots, sometimes snipped the thread, and at times poked the needle to untangle it. Each emotion brought with it a wave of memories and emotions. It is said that one should rip off a bandage to lessen the physical pain. Here I was taking off the bandage, little by little, feeling every pinch and pain in my emotional state. It was difficult and exhausting but a necessary process.

I had once read how Jain saints pluck their hair as a mark of renunciation of worldly pleasures during a ritual called *Kesh Lochan*. Herein, each strand of hair is pulled off their head to go through the suffering till they become bald.

I felt I was doing something similar, this was *'Bhavlochan'*. It took me a few months but I went through each emotion and purified my system.

Healing happens in layers like an onion. You peel yourself layer by layer and surprisingly, whichever emotion or feeling appears at that moment confirms that it has surfaced because it is now ready to be healed.

It was a process which I had begun to go through, like being naked in my soul and ready to open my wounds to be healed, gradually and with care and kindness towards myself. I trusted the natural progress to feel safe and secure during unfolding and closing the many aspects of my fragmented self until it completed itself and I was ready to integrate all my lost soul portions and live gracefully.

Scars tell a story of the journey of a being,
They hold memories from the past to present,
Scars are stitched wounds that reflect the struggles and
victories alike,
Few who befriend their shadows gather the nerve to show
their scars,
Scars contain, confirm and remain mystery of the wisdom
gained.

Both Pritam and I were growing. I spiritually, he financially, and together we were growing apart.

During our trip to London, I noticed that he was more interested in buying gifts for Radhika at Harrods, rather than enjoying and shopping with the family. On a trip to the United States, Pritam was constantly on the phone with Radhika.

Goa was a revelation for me. There, I realised how important Radhika was for Pritam. We had gone to Goa with two more couples, both were Pritam's friends, but one call from Radhika was enough for him to cut short the holiday and fly back to her. It was embarrassing, yet everyone chose to remain silent.

I wonder if similar behaviour would have been accepted if it had been me. Why do we try to ignore when a marriage falters? Why is it that family and friends refrain from resolving the issue thinking it best to not interfere or intrude? Why do we prefer to gossip rather than offer help?

In most cases of divorce the man and woman easily tell everyone how horrible the partner had been, ruined his or her life, was mean to their mother or probably left them for another person. All the relatives and friends then gather and shame the spouse, blaming them for ruining and breaking the marriage. It is a convenient and accepted escape. No one pauses to understand that a marriage breaks because of incompatibility and lack of mutual respect.

It was clear by now that Pritam wanted to control everything and he was good at it, for controlling is nothing but a mind game. He could manipulate and exploit not just people but also situations, skills he had inherited and mastered over the years.

I had often heard that men controlled with money and women with emotions but in the true essence of control, you cannot control anyone or anything other than yourself. I could control my thoughts, words, behaviour and feelings but not the other person's. This is the same with everyone. One can only influence the other. Unless you give permission, nobody can control you. Yes, they may have to employ other methods such as abuse, force or manipulation to control your behaviour and extract a reaction desirable for them.

As Veena could not change herself, Pritam or me, she began to manipulate Pritam, encourage Radhika and ill-treat me. Pritam chose to be manipulated for he willingly listened to her speak poorly about me. It is easy to say that Veena controlled her son but the fact is that she only influenced him. Ultimately, it was his choice if he chose to misbehave with me or cheat on me. Similarly, I could not control Pritam's feelings for either himself or Radhika. It was clear that Pritam and Radhika loved each other and wanted to spend more time together. She knew his personal and professional passwords, he got her whatever she wanted, fought for her and even gave her a set of keys to his personal locker in the office.

I had never needed a man or marriage to fulfil my life. I always knew that if and when I had a man in my life, it would be a peaceful and respectful relationship held in trust. I did have a man in my life but the beautiful relationship of marriage with that man had become ugly and bitter. I was ready to let go of it. I knew it through my soul's cry and the spirits had conveyed it to me, loud and clear.

Every word you say goes out to the Universe and what you write once, you remember forever. I had already written my story exactly as I had wanted in the Akashic Records. I could now pay multiple visits to that divine time and space when I had penned it down. Everything had become still in that moment of movement. The magic had started working. I did not need any more proof that our marriage had been long over. It was time for me to move on.

"How and why should I stay where I was not wanted?" I had asked Farida and myself many times.

"That is for you to figure out, Tara, and also how the abuses are serving you to stay put in this bond?" she asked. "Whom you are giving the baton to matters more than who is passing it to you. The entire game can change in that split second between the handing and taking over of the baton for that moment is of trust, choice and responsibility. In the pass over, you are the connector."

One of us had to be bold enough to rock the boat and make the shift. The moment I realised that there had to be a catalyst, I recalled the words of the High Priestess, "If not for yourself, then for whom? If not now, then when?"

My inner voice said, "Stay with me, stay connected. Get deeper to fly higher, to get connected to the higher vibrations." Now, there was no past to return to. First, I needed to retrieve my beliefs before I could act. Earlier, I used to say, "life changed me." Now I chose to say, "I dared to change my life."

That day during meditation, I handed over the reins of my relationship with Pritam to the One I trusted completely, Lord Shiva. I let it go as Sri Krishna had said in the *Gita*,

*"Sarvadharmānparityajya māmekā śarāā vraja
Ahā tvā sarvapāpebhyo moksayiāyāmi mā śucāh"*

(Abandoning all *Dharmas* - of the body, mind and intellect - take refuge in Me alone; I will liberate thee from all sins; grieve not.)

As the wedding season started, Delhi saw a number of exhibitions. A friend wanted to visit an exhibition that was happening at a five-star hotel and asked me to come along. While there, I heard whispers that His Holiness, the Dalai Lama, was staying at the hotel. As we were going down in the elevator, I asked a hotel employee who confirmed the news.

We had reached the ground floor and were walking towards the lobby. Despite being discouraged by my friend to enquire further, I mustered up courage to request the hotel employee if we could meet His Holiness. Just as I made my request, he received a call on his phone that His Holiness was entering the hotel. Surprised at the timing of the call, he smiled and said, "I do not believe in these things but it seems like a sign. His Holiness has entered the premises. You may wait for him at the entrance and try your luck."

That morning, Anupama, my childhood friend, had sent me a message that said, "Life is like a fairy tale, full of mysteries, whose end is an open secret and yet, each day holds magic."

Remembering the words she had sent, I walked excitedly towards the entrance where dozens of people were waiting in the large lobby to get a glimpse of His Holiness or a chance to meet him. Just as I reached, His Holiness entered, I looked at him and he looked directly into my eyes. I bowed to receive his blessings.

He patted my cheek and offered his hand to me. I held it and walked with him a few steps before introducing my friend and her daughter to him. He blessed them both and retired to his room. I just stood there, dazed. Every time I experienced emotional turmoil that left me weak, vulnerable or doubting, His Holiness had graced me with his presence. In his aura, I was able to receive clarity and strength. With each meeting, I felt something inside me shifted, which unfolded the mystery of the future.

"God has prepared a path for everyone to follow.
You just have to read the omens that he left for you."
- The Alchemist by Paulo Coelho

There is an element of hopelessness when you hope.
A probability of failure with success.

Dear Diary,

There is nothing more beautiful than when you prove to
yourself just how strong you are

My pen stopped.

Why is it necessary to prove strength to oneself?

Why is it considered beautiful?

As I questioned this further, I wondered if I was taking pride in being strong and probably that was massaging my ego to create new challenges to attract and then overcome.

I suddenly realised that I had created this loop and had got myself involved in it all this while.

"Oh my God!" I thought, unable to control my laughter.

I realised that living in an abusive relationship was adding new challenges in my life. That made life interesting, massaged the ego to overcome it and made me believe that it was giving meaning to my life by being a perfectionist and an idealist.

This was a loop I had created to pat my back.

Dear Diary,

There is nothing more beautiful than when you prove to

~~yourself just how strong you are~~

I was stuck in the 'Matrix' of multiple games by the Superior Intelligence and I was playing it well as per the role allotted to me. Now I choose the role.

- Realised
* Tara*

WISH, for they come true,
Wishes COME true.

> *Dear Diary,*
>
> *It is easier to write that the marriage had ended and I was ready to let it go, but it was not easy. It took me years to even acknowledge the reality, let alone act on it for this was a man I had fallen in love with, built a home with and shared the most part of my life with. Ironically, I got married at the age of twenty-one and had been married for twenty-one years. There were days when I doubted if I was right. My gut knew and my soul had known for long now but my mind made me wonder if I was making the right decision.*
>
> *Mind games. Uff! How the mind loves to keep us busy in a loop, confused and wondering. The mind is like a monkey. One day, I will train it and take charge.*
>
> *- Monkey trainer*
> *Tara*

During this time, I met a Sufi in Rishikesh. Clad in white, he was in the surrendered state and merged with the One. With a *Sufiana nazariya*, he would raise his hands to praise and thank the Almighty after every sentence, referring to the Divine as "*Aap*".

Sitting in front of him, I found solace and yet, the moment he kept his hand on my head, tears rolled down.

Singing praises for the Lord, he stopped suddenly, looked into my eyes and said, "*Nafratein bhi wahi paida karta hai dillon mein aur mohabbatein bhi.*" (It is Him, the Almighty, who creates both love and hatred in our hearts)

He smiled at me, as if reading my mind, and continued, "Surrender and accept the offering from the One. What the spirits desire, spirits attain. Ask what you want and it shall be granted."

I closed my eyes while receiving the message and bowed my head.

The best feeling in the world is being loved back by the person you love. Remember, when you forgive, you heal. And when you let go, you grow.

In one of the classes a Shaman said, "Ask and it shall be granted. If you ask with fear, the returns come laden with fears. Ask with faith and it shall be provided."

In a TED Talk, I heard about the power of energy, "Turn up, create, tune-in and set a powerful frequency to love. What you say, you become. Stay focused on the highest version of what you want. Shift your energy and surround yourself with forces which make you leap, stretch you and make you feel happy. Be aware of people who drain your energies or do not inspire you."

I anchored into the higher vibrations and the right frequency to become the nucleus of my destiny. I started reading on, 'how to muster courage to lead your own life', 'how to plan a separation', and 'how to keep oneself calm in a toxic relationship', amongst other such topics. With Farida, our topics of discussion had shifted from what and why to how and when. I had lost many battles only to win the war of respect. I had often prayed for love, strength, clarity and death during times of extreme distress, and now, for the right moment.

It is said that one should not make promises casually which

cannot be upheld. Such promises could mean everything for the other person and they get bound by the promise, strangulating both sides.

As a child, I had heard Maa say, "Do not promise if you cannot commit and fulfil." In spirituality, the same words were reiterated and I understood their importance now. Promises should never be taken lightly for once made, they get imprinted on your soul and hold a Karmic story. Most promises were made out of love or grief and these were the worst for it could take a person multiple births to fulfil them. As I was letting go of the most important part of my identity till now, I also let go of every promise made to Pritam and to myself as I did not want to suffer with the burden of living with it.

I witnessed the shift in my life. Now, I had to make the choice - when to take the last leap, the tactical leap! I remembered the Priestess' words, "Warrior-*Yogini*".

Trust the timing of life events, they have a reason.

I enjoyed spending time on my terrace, basking in the early morning Sun feeling relaxed and calm. I was ready to welcome the new feeling of letting go. I saw eagles flying high and free flowing together. Slowly, they started descending and one eagle attracted my attention as it came and perched on a rod emerging from the roof of the neighbour's house. It fluttered its wings and took flight.

"Please show me a sign if the path I have chosen is correct for me. A sign is all I need," I said looking at the eagle, the sky and beyond it, to the Universe. There was a moment of silence and sudden stillness, as if the message was being delivered and then suddenly the wind blew and I heard windchimes from a distance. The eagle took a turn towards the terrace and a feather detached from it.

My eyes locked in on the feather as it flew with the rhythm of the gentle wind and to my astonishment, it fell in front of me. I screamed. I was shocked and in awe. Slowly, I gathered the courage to touch the feather, to check if it was real. The moment I bent down to pick it, the High Priestess appeared in front of me and touched my forehead with a blessing. By the time I looked up, the Priestess had vanished.

The moment of truth hit me. The whole world seemed to pause and I was there, living in the moment of stillness.

Calm, in control, connected to my breath and the One, aligned all together.

I thanked the eagle and the Priestess for their blessings. I was liberated. I covered the feather along with the gift from Ida Ayu in a red silk cloth and kept it safely.

I trusted the present and stopped worrying about the future. I was out of the relationship which had nothing to offer or contribute. The time had arrived and the timing was right.

That night, I had an out-of-body experience. As I was sleeping, I felt that I was floating upward. Suddenly, I saw my dead body lying in front of me and as I moved ahead, I heard voices. I could not make out if they were people, spirits or shadows but they were flipping pages of a large book. It looked like a book of records and they seemed to be searching for something. They stopped turning the pages, as one of them read my name out loud. All of a sudden, a shadow glided from my right, almost brushing my shoulder, and rushed towards them screaming, "Stop! Do not announce her name. She has altered her destiny. Send her back. It says here that she has to live more."

A re-check was done, the book was closed and my soul was blown back into my body.

I woke up with a sudden shock, gasping for breath, trying to process what had just happened.

"Life is not measured by the number of breaths we take but by the moments that take our breaths away." - Maya Angelou

It is said that eleven is the number of angels. Eleven days after I received the feather, I was at my favourite spot by the window at a café. It was raining outside and I had just finished my chocolate croissant but there was something in that moment that I did not want to leave the café and decided to repeat my cup of flat white. I crossed a little blackboard on the wall which read, "Have faith, miracles happen," and stood in the queue behind a grey-haired man.

"One flat white, medium. I'll pay by card, please."

I gasped. It had been eleven years since I had heard that voice.

"Shiv?"

Three hours later we were still at the café, catching up from where we had left off last. Nothing had changed between us except the greys in the hair, a little more wisdom and a new outlook towards life. After so long, it felt like home. There was childlike excitement and joy.

"Kehte hain na, kuch log aur cheezein ruh ko khush kar deti hain (It is said that some people and some things bring joy to the soul)."

As I drove back, I was happy and could not stop laughing. I did not know what to do or whom to share it with. In my excitement, I jumped a traffic signal and got *challaned*. As soon as I reached home, I ran to my room and took out the feathers, the gift from the eagle and the High Priestess. Today, I learnt to say no and yes at the right time. The time had changed and shifted into the new space.

I opened my diary eager to write about my meeting with Shiv, picked up my pen and brought it to paper.

Dear Diary,

- Zipped
Tara

I closed the diary without writing anything. I was a communicator and connector. For me words mattered and yet, that day I felt limited to put down my experience and capture it in words. I savoured the meeting and held it close to my heart, not wanting to share it with anyone.

I was restless and yet, at peace for the next two days. Restless as if I had to hurry up to go somewhere, and at peace as if I knew all is fine. This time I had saved Shiv's number under a friend's name. Neither of us called or messaged each other. I knew Pritam and his reaction if he found out. This time, I had to be cautious but confident.

That evening, my shower stretched to an hour as I simply wanted to relive the memory of my meeting with Shiv again and again. I replayed the sentences, paused them, felt them, sensed them and observed from another perspective, and played them again.

I did not know if we would meet again or not and a part of me did not care, for I was happy and content in that moment.

So, I left it to Shiva with a smile, in full faith and complete trust as He knew what was best for me.

"What you seek is seeking you." - Rumi

Ishq aur mushq chhupaye nahi chhupte.

"Do you love him, Tara?" Farida asked.

"What do you mean?" I counter-questioned her, almost defensively.

"Love is simply love, Tara, and you of all people should not be asking me this question. You either feel it or you do not. There are no in-betweens. It is us who have given labels such as like, love and infatuation. We have assigned "appropriate degrees" of love that is allowed to be given based on who it is, a boyfriend-girlfriend, offspring, partner, sibling, parent, friend or whoever else," Farida replied.

There was a constant smile on my face and my laughter had returned. I continued to ignore my feelings for Shiv and focused on simply feeling happy and fulfilled. Shiv and I kept meeting whenever we could, racing up in our respective cars to have a *paan* in Connaught Place.

The *saada paan* on *meetha patta* was the best with a little bit of *khushboo, chutney, elaichi, geeli supari* and *lachha*. The trick was that the fresh betel leaf had to be cut properly and seasoned with the right amount of *katha* and *chuna*. Bansi, owner of the *paan* shop was a storyteller. He taught us how to place the *paan* in the corner of the mouth to relish it for a long time.

It was in these little moments that Shiv and I found comfort and joy. Sitting on the wooden bench, listening to this wise man talk passionately about the famous and influential people who had visited him and how every customer had personal taste and individual style for their *paan*.

Over the years Bansi had become good at guessing the personality of the buyer by their choice of *paan* and ingredients.

I laughed and asked him what he thought about us.

Bansi looked at Shiv and me and said, "*Abhi bhi mohobbat hai*," and handed me my special *paan* with a smile.

"*Aap poochh rahein hain ya bata rahein hain*?" I asked.

"*Jo aap samajhna chahein*," he said, with a soft smile and a twinkle in his eyes.

On certain days, we would grab a ride on the *tonga*. Raja was a handsome horse of his proud master, Aslam whose great-grandfather was the first to start the *tonga* rides in Chandni Chowk. After independence, they could be seen in Connaught Place as well, especially in front of the Marina Hotel, now Radisson Blu.

Pritam was usually busy with Radhika and the office or out of town. We rarely talked to each other. Veena was happy till the time Pritam and I were out of the house separately.

I would surprise Shiv in his office or meet him at our favourite café and relish coffee with an extra shot of espresso. I did not tell anyone about Shiv lest it caught a jealous eye. I wanted to preserve and cherish every moment of it, all for myself.

"Travel and tell no one,
Live a true love story and tell no one,
Live happily and tell no one,
People ruin beautiful things."
- Kahlil Gibran

Meeting Shiv had raised my happiness quotient and confidence back in myself. Each day passed with no attachments of past hardships or future worries. Hopelessness of the past was replaced by peace in the present.

As expected, my friends and clients saw the change in my approach towards life, words and actions. The news reached Pritam, who had been getting suspicious of my constant smile and carefree laughter.

I had forgotten that if fear was one of the nine emotions, so was courage.

A detective started following me again.

Being devotees of Shiva, we often visited temples together. On one such day, I felt someone following us. As I folded my hands in front of the deity, I knew that time had arrived with divine timing.

This was the catalyst.

With folded hands I looked straight into the eyes of Shiva and Shakti and asked for their blessings for strength. At that very moment, I visualised myself walking into the idol of Ma Durga and calmly sat inside her.

I surrendered. I was protected and ready.

Shiv had no idea about the intensity and gravity of the situation. He never asked, I never disclosed. We were engrossed in enjoying every meeting and every moment of togetherness. I knew he was not the reason behind my decision to end the relationship with Pritam.

That evening I overheard Pritam advising his friend, "Never disclose about your affair or interest in a woman to your wife. If she creates a scene, give her a tight slap and stop giving her money. She will understand who the boss is and shut up. Bloody women who feel they can command everyone and the idiotic men who actually believe that women can do so. I hate these new-age bold women with an independent mind and useless bastards who think women are equal. Change your masks smartly and use women wisely. They are supposed to serve us for our desires."

Pritam was confident that he "could sort Tara out". Pritam had returned to his roots and I had retrieved mine. I was happy that I had completed everything I was assigned to in this soul contract. Now, it was time to exit.

The exit had to be at the right time, ensuring that I gave my best to the marriage and nothing less than that.

That night, in a separate room, I opened my diary and for the first time I wrote about everything I contributed to this marriage:

Dear Diary,

My contribution to this marriage with my (once) Pritam:

1. *Married against all odds*
2. *Made a beautiful home*
3. *Started small, walked through challenges*
4. *Started and expanded business(es)*
5. *Freed Pritam from trivial matters and let him soar high*
6. *Raised the children*
7. *Looked after my in-laws*
8. *Received abuses, insults but held strong*
9. *Forgave Pritam for his infidelities*
10. *Accepted his love for Radhika*

11. Had beautiful spiritual experiences and learning

12. Tried everything to save the marriage.

13. Had courage to move out when the purpose of marriage was complete

14. ....

- Sincerely

Tara

I stopped at #14 as by then I felt that I had done everything I could in my capacity and capability.

Now, being the Warrior-*Yogini*, I had to be ready to defend and protect myself and raise the weapon, when required.

For me, the principles had to be strong, rules could bend. Pritam played to win. His ego was hurt and wounded. This time, I thanked Pritam for initiating action. He set the ball rolling and now even he could not stop what was to come. He had broken all principles and shown the worst of what he could become. He thought that by distancing Shiv and maligning me, everything would go back to being normal, his normal. Pritam would never acknowledge the fact that Shiv was never the problem. The marriage had ended long ago.

The war had begun!

Pritam brought the family together, children and parents, in one room and ordered, "Apologise to my parents and me and I will accept you back. You will never see Shiv or hear from him again. What you have seen is just a trailer. I will tarnish your image and ruin you. I will tear you apart. You will have to sleep with men for money as I ensure you are left penniless and faceless.

You will be cut-off from friends and family. You will lose the privilege of being a rich man's wife. You will not be able to go for foreign trips, parties and vacations. All my friends cheat but their wives stay on quietly. How dare you leave me? I give you one last opportunity to apologise. Live on my terms and I shall accept you back. Remember, you are nothing without me," he howled.

While Pritam was talking, a vision appeared in front of my eyes. The Warrior-*Yogini* had come alive. The time had come to take the last leap.

I felt bad that he had gathered the family for this outburst. It was unfortunate that our kids had to witness it but it was a choice Pritam made, as always. So be it.

Integrating all my soul parts, I called upon the spirits and guides and *Mahadev* to be with me. I looked straight into

Pritam's eyes and said, "We married against all odds. We had a beautiful relationship of love and respect. We both know that we have changed individually as well as with each other. You know that your mother always hated me. You stood for my rights initially, but then you stopped. You not only turned against me but you crossed the line, insulted me, abused me and cheated on me.

It is evident that you and Radhika are in love and your mother supports that relationship. Then why this drama? I don't think that a third party is needed to resolve our problems when we have grown apart. I do not like the person you have become and you have not liked me for years, then why this façade? I cannot stay for the sake of society or others. The choices made by the wives of your friends are their own. Their life is not ours. It does not matter if there is Radhika, Shiv or your mother. The fact is that we are not together anymore. The truth is that we had stopped being a couple long ago.

Look within you, Pritam. You let the worst in you overpower your own goodness. You are helpful and a giver but that does not make you God. You lost your humility somewhere. You lack grace. You have no emotions, Pritam. For you, it is just a game of manipulation. Any man with decency would not use the words that you have used for any woman and any woman with pride would not have stayed with a man who had disgraced her.

We both know that our relationship is dead and just as one does not carry or keep a dead body for long, we need to let go of this relationship too. I free you of this deceased relationship as I free myself from it. Thank you for being my partner in this life and space. Without you, I would not have tread the spiritual path. I take full responsibility to close and complete this marriage. Goodbye, Pritam."

I knew that it was now or never. It was easier for me to walk the familiar path. The unknown would be difficult but I was ready for it.

In that moment of truth, I closed my eyes, listened to my heart, trusted my gut feeling, strengthened my mind, stood up and walked out of the room. I left the present space, the place which had disrespected my being, the place where my pride and womanhood were insulted. For years, I had lived and died here, many times.

There was silence, complete silence behind me. The purpose of this marriage was fulfilled.

As I walked out, I felt heaviness leaving me. In that moment I moved into the Light waiting across, as if entering a new womb ready to experience new life. For me, the journey had always been more important than the destination. I did not know where the road led, but I would make sure I lived each day to the fullest, and in the company of those who loved and respected me for who I was.

I felt the strength of 'letting go' flow through me.

I remembered Nisargadatta Maharaj's words in the book, *I Am That*, "To know what you want, first find out what you do not want." I did not want disrespect, abuse, rejection, hatred, anger and deception. I knew I wanted, a respectful, compassionate, healthy and happy life, a life full of thriving relationships.

Standing in front of the mirror, I looked into my eyes and smiled.

Jis pal tum meri aankhon se khud ko dekhoge,
Khuda ki kasam, khud se mohabbat ho jayegi

(The moment you see yourself through my eyes, I swear by the Almighty, you will fall in love with yourself)

After so many years, I slept peacefully that night. I had crossed over. Maybe, the journey was not so much about becoming. Maybe, it was about unbecoming everything that was not the real me.

In my sleep, I saw myself carrying a huge backpack walking on a railway station. I removed the heavy load and left it on the tracks and boarded the nearest train.

Sometimes, the people you want as part of your story are only meant to be chapters.

The next morning, I went to the office to collect my things. I met Radhika. "Hello, Radhika. I know you wanted to own the company. Now, you have the Company and Pritam. It is all yours. All the best," I said and left.

That evening, Veena, surreptitiously entered my bedroom and said, "What is this drama going on? Why are you creating a scene? You have a good life, money and servants. You never got anything in dowry, still you are living like a Queen. What more do you want?"

I smiled and said, "Please do not mock either of us with these words. You always hated me and our marriage. You do not have any right over me as you never gained the trust of being a mother. You must be happy so please do not put on an act of concern. Please leave my room. I am leaving your son and now he is all yours."

At around 2:30 A.M. I heard a knock on the door. I opened it and found Pritam standing there. I closed the door.

The next day I left to attend the Kumbh Mela.

"She was brave
and strong
and broken
all at once."
- Anna Funder

"We believe that God sees us from above but he actually sees us from the inside." - Shams Tabrizi

Attending the Kumbh Mela was an event of becoming one with the flow and then becoming the flow itself, and following signs from the above.

Although I was one to stay away from crowded places or events, this time, I said yes as soon as my friend invited me to attend the Kumbh Mela. We boarded a train from Delhi to Allahabad, now Prayagraj, to witness the biggest pilgrimage where devotees take a dip in the holy *sangam* (confluence of rivers, the Ganges, the Yamuna and the Saraswati). It is considered a sacred event for Hindus, where devotees from all over the world attend. The dip in the cold water of the river is considered a test of a person's devotion.

I was excited but no longer nervous of the crowd. I had let go of my fear of the unknown. I wanted to experience the grandeur of the event. As we reached the city, we made our way to the river. The moment I stepped on the banks, I felt a pull. I knew I was meant to be here, in this moment. I, the one who detested crowds, suddenly became one amongst the thousands present there.

As we were returning to the camp, one of us expressed interest to witness the parade of the Naga Sadhus to take the holy dip at the *sangam* on the pious occasion of *Mauni*

Amavasya the next morning. This happens to be one of the most revered events at the Kumbh Mela.

The next morning, we reached the area at around 3:30 A.M. to witness the biggest event of the Mela. We found a spot from where the Naga Sadhus would begin their journey. I had brought a blanket to survive the cold morning. I could see many Naga Sadhus who were already there and many more were coming in groups. The area was full of pilgrims.

As we continued to wait in the cold, I said to my friend, "We should have brought tea."

Just then, we heard a voice from behind, "*Garam chai.*" I turned around and saw a man selling hot tea in paper cups.

My friend looked at me with surprise, and I smiled in gratitude.

After half an hour, the police came to clear the passage for the Sadhus and all the onlookers standing there were moved away. As everyone emptied the area, the police ushered my friends to the side but did not move me.

I stood there like a statue. The path was being cleared, the police kept moving around me, as if I was invisible, clearing everyone in the area, except me.

And then the parade began.

I could see the Nagas approaching. It was like a wave of people who swept me along with them. Before I could comprehend the situation, I had become a part of the Sadhus, walking with them and chanting while moving towards the holy water.

The number of people around me increased. It was growing bigger, larger and crazier. Loud slogans for Shiva were being chanted. "Shiva, the *Mahadev*, the one who never took birth and never died." He had conquered all the virtues and vices and was beyond time and space. It is said that the one who finds Shiva has achieved *moksha* or liberation from the loop of life, death and rebirth.

"*Har Har Mahadev, Har Har Mahadev, Har Har Mahadev*", the chants grew louder and louder. The *sanyasis, sanyasinis, yogis* and *yoginis*, everyone joined in the congregation to take the first dip with the Naga Sadhus.

The ceremony to become a Naga Sadhu is very tough and to remain one is even more challenging and difficult. They go through different stages of indoctrination under their *gurus* and take oaths never to return to civilisation. They give up all worldly and materialistic desires, and take a vow of celibacy. They remain naked and in union with the One. They possess nothing and are wedded to the Divine. With ash smeared all over their bodies, they are an integral and an important part of the Kumbh Mela. That year women Nagas were seen at the Mela for the first time. They were emanating power with a strong aura.

Amidst the chorus, rhythm, unity, devotion and surrender, I had started feeling claustrophobic and nauseous. It was way too crowded for me and I felt like giving up. I was thirsty, and between the loud chants, smell of *dhuni* and thousands of *sadhus*, I was losing myself.

I looked to my right, wondering if I should step out, when an elderly *sadhu* appeared in front of me. He looked into my eyes and said, "Keep moving, do not give up. Keep moving *Betiya*, keep moving!" He threw a saffron cloth at me, I blinked, and he vanished. I looked around but could not see him anywhere.

I continued walking and as I crossed the bridge, suddenly there was a strong push which threw me towards a rope on the side and I fell. A security personnel on duty helped me stand up and looked at me with concern. As if able to read my mind, he suggested that I step out. "This is not meant for you, Ma'am. It is too crowded. How come you are here?"

I stood there, contemplating if I should continue or not when the *sadhu* reappeared. As if shaking me out of this confusion, he pulled me back into the crowd and commanded that I should not give up and keep moving. Surprised at his sudden reappearance, I took a deep breath and inhaled the smell of *dhuni,* this time to give me strength and not weaken me.

Considering it another omen, I held the *rudraksha mala* tightly in my left hand and I continued, focusing on the path and the destination ahead as the chants of 'Har Har Mahadev' filled the air. It was as if my being was swept by the wave of *Sadhus*, a force beyond my control. Before I knew, we had reached the banks of the holy *sangam*.

Helicopters showered rose petals on the revered sea of the Nagas. It was beautiful and surreal. I took my first step wilfully and consciously. As the water touched my feet, there was awareness of just being and being alive.

The water was freezing and I was ready. On the first dip,

I felt physical pain leaving my body. With the second, I released the fears residing within me. As I took the third dip, memories of insults, rejections and a part of myself that was not serving well to the soul exited. I stopped counting and kept on diving in and out of the water till everything that was dead and decayed in me got washed away. It was as if all emotions and burdens that were not conducive to the journey of my soul were extracted and discarded in the confluence of the three rivers.

The last dip cleansed my soul, body and mind. I stood up and saw my *mala* being taken away by the Ganges. I let it go. I turned around towards the river bank and started walking, feeling lighter and engulfed in the Light.

The layers which had dimmed my inner strength and eroded parts of my being had been washed off. I felt as if I was born again, a new life was granted to me to be myself.

"Between what is said and not meant, and what is meant and not said, most of love is lost." - Kahlil Gibran

One month later I moved out of the marriage, regret-free. As I walked out, I left the good and the bad memories behind me. I stepped into an unknown zone with a clean slate of possibilities. I was now free to create anew.

As a believer in the Supreme Power, I had come to an understanding that a sublime power resided in me too. I realised that everything happened in its own course of time and space. The power within me often merged with the divine and I would not only flow but become the flow. It was in being in alignment with the One that I felt connected and grounded, both simultaneously. I would pray and surrender to the Supreme Will, not in wait, judgement or denial but in trust. I would merge with the One and know that the rest would be taken care of.

I noticed that the moment I let my mind talk, fear and doubt galloped back and the outcome faltered. So, I trusted my instinct and followed the signs. It is my ardent belief that the Universe shows signs to everyone but we are too occupied in our old patterns, perceptions and understanding that we do not notice them. If you look carefully, in silence, within yourself and observe, everyone would be able to see the omens.

Today, I walk across the fire with no fear, doubt, shame or guilt. I am free with no knowledge of what the future will hold, with faith by my side.

The one thing I am certain of is a desire to grow, learn and evolve. I am ready to lead my life my way.

I learnt that, *"Mohabbat ho jati hai, shaadi kee jaati hai, aur alag bhi hua jata hai."*

That night, in bed, a message flashed on my phone, "I am learning to love the sound of my feet walking away from the things not meant for me."

"Yet another sign," I thought, smiling. I bowed in gratitude.

I believe that even if we could not live happily forever at least we can live peacefully even after.

In freeing Pritam, I liberated myself.

Leave behind what you have to, to move ahead where you want to.

- Tara

"The world you perceive is made of consciousness; what you call matter is consciousness itself. You are the space in which it moves, the time in which it lasts, the love that gives it life."
- Shree Nisargadatta Maharaj

Aap poochh rahein hain ya bata rahein hain?: Are you asking or telling?
Abhi bhi mohobbat hai: Love is still there
Agni Pariksha: Ordeal of fire
Aham Brahmasmi: I am the creator
Ajna Chakra: Third eye
Amavasya: No moon day
Anahat: Heart *chakra*
Atma Gyan: Knowledge about the self
Aurat ko hi chup rehna padhta hai. Aadmi jaat aisi hi hoti hai: Men are the way
they are. Women should keep quiet
Baba: Father
Basant: Spring
Betiya: Daughter
Bhagavad Gita: One of the holy books of Hinduism
Bhaiya: Brother
Bhakt: Devotee
Bhav: Emotion
Bhed: Division
Bhelpuri: Indian street food
Bindi: A mark worn or drawn in the middle of the forehead
Brahmacharya: Path to divinity wherein a person lets go of every
material and social pleasures of life, including practicing sexual celibacy
Buri nazar wale tera muh kaala: Phrase used to ward off evil eye
Chakra: Subtle energy centres in the body
Challan: Fine issued for a legal violation
Chole Bhature: Indian street food
Daam: Negotiation
Dadi: Paternal grandmother
Dal: Indian dish made with pulses
Dand: Punishment
Darti kyun ho? Jaano tum kaun ho. Shakti ho! Sone ki tarah mazboot bano aur chamko. Daro nahi. Ma Durga tumhare saath hai, tum surakshit ho: Why do you fear? Know who you are. You are strength.
Be strong like gold and shine! Do not be scared. Goddess Durga is with
you. You are protected
Deva: God
Devraja: King of Gods
Devshakti Queen of Gods
Dharma: Moral duty

Dhuni: Sacred smoke

Diwali: Hindu festival of lights

Diya: Oil lamp

Doordarshan: Indian television channel

Dukh ko itni jagah mat do ki dard ban jaye: Do not give so much space to your sorrow that it becomes pain

Dupatta: Type of scarf

Gamcha: Thin cotton towel

Garam Chai: Hot tea

Guru: Spiritual teacher

Har Har Mahadev: Chant to Lord Shiva for protection and liberation from sorrows

Himsa: Violence

Ishq aur mushq chhupaye nahi chhupte: Love and fragrance cannot be hidden

Jain: Adherent of Jainism

Jis pal tum meri aankhon se khud ko dekhoge; Khuda ki kasam, khud se mohabbat ho jayegi: The moment you see yourself through my eyes, I swear by the Almighty, you will fall in love with yourself

Jo aap samajhna chahein: Whatever you want to think

Jo kar, so bhar: As you sow, so shall you reap

Kamandal: Pot-like vessel used to carry water

Karma: Action

Kehte hain log ki hum khush mijazi hain; Hum bhi bol pade, Yeh toh upar wale ki mehr hai, dost, Warna kiski rooh nahi kaampi aur aansu jholi mein na aye: People say that I am a happy soul. "This is a blessing of God, otherwise no one is spared from bad times and everyone gets scared," I replied

Kehte hain na, kuch log aur cheezein ruh ko khush kar deti hain: It is said that some people and some things bring joy to the soul

Kesh Lochan: A ritual of plucking hair from the scalp as mark of renunciation of worldly pleasures

Khaadi: A hand-spun and woven cotton fabric

Kootniti: Diplomacy

Kota: A city in Rajasthan, India

Krishna Consciousness: State of awareness

Kumbh Mela: A religious festival of Hindus held every three years

Loban: Form of incense

Lokas: Reference of different worlds in Hinduism

Maa: Mother

Mahadev: Lord Shiva

Mala: String of beads

Mandir: Temple

Manipurna: Solar plexus

Mantra: Word/s repeated frequently

Mauni: Silence

Meetha: Sweet

Mohabbat ho jati hai, shaadi kee jaati hai, aur alag bhi hua jata hai:
Love happens, marriage is a social commitment that takes place and
separation can be a choice

Moksha: Liberation from the cycle of life and death

Muladhar: Root *chakra*

Muni: Ascetic

Nafratein bhi wahi paida karta hai dillo mein aur mohabbatein bhi: It
is Him, the Almighty, who creates both love and hatred in our hearts

Naga Sadhus: Followers of Lord Shiva

Namaste mudra: Hand gesture with both palms touching each other

Narak: Hell

Paan: Indian preparation made with betel leaves, includes assorted
mouth fresheners, digestives, fragrance/tobacco

Pallu: Loose end of a *saree*

Patta: Leaf

Raja: King

Raja Shakti Queen

Roti: Type of bread

Rudraksha: Natural prayer beads

Saada: Plain

Saam: Equality

Sadhu: Ascetic

Sahasara: Crown *chakra*

Sangam: Confluence of rivers

Sanyasi/Sanyasini: Men and women who follow *Sanyas*, a form of
asceticism

Saree: Dress worn by South Asian women

Satsang: Religious gathering where hymns and devotional songs are
sung

Shakti: Strength; Goddess

Shanti: Internal peace

Shastra: Sacred scripture

Shunya: State of nothing or zeroness

Sindoor: Vermillion

Sufiana Nazariya: Saintly attitude

Sukh: External material gains

Svetambara: Jain muni who wear white clothes

Swadishthan: Sacral *chakra*

Swarg: Heaven

Tantrik: Practitioner of *Tantra*
Tapasya: Penance
Tehkhana: Cellar
Tonga: A two-wheeled vehicle drawn by horse/s
Tu khilona hai mere liye. Jaise jee chahega, waise rakhoonga. Chhodhne ki koshish kari toh dekhna kya karunga: You are a toy for me. I will treat you the way I want. You cannot even imagine what I will do if you try to leave me
Vishuddhi: Throat *chakra*
Vriti: Archetype
Yajna: Sacred fire ceremony
Yama or Yama Raja: Hindu God of Death
Yama Shakti: Hindu Goddess of Death
Yogi/Yogini: Practitioner of *Yoga* (male/female)

About the Author

Vibha's lifetime commitment to guiding others on their spiritual path is an inspiration to many and a testament of her dedication to her craft.

Beginning with two Bachelors' degrees, one in Sociology and another in Education through her Post Graduate Diploma in Journalism and Master's degree in Political Science, Vibha Gurtu has always sought truth and knowledge in areas that help her assist others in their process of growth.

After having trained in reiki, pranic healing, hypnotherapy and other holistic healing modalities, Vibha has been a practioner and facilitator of Shamanism since 2013. She founded Aumtara Trust in New Delhi, a closely knitted group of spiritualists, healers, energy channels and coaches. Through Aumtara, Vibha works on aligning inner awareness with outer realities, guiding her clients to heal and overcome physical, mental, emotional, and spiritual traumas.

For over 20 years as a soul coach, spiritual guide and image consultant, Vibha has worked with numerous individuals to assist them in finding their true potential by unlocking both their inner and outer power. She is passionate about guiding her clients and helping them heal from the traumas that hold them back from achieving their highest potential.

To learn more, visit
www.vibhagurtu.com

Castle Mount
— Media —
2023

"Improving Leadership & Communication
In Business, Healthcare, & Education"

Castle Mount Media GmbH & Co. KG is a publishing
company located in Erlangen, Germany, which specializes
in print and digital media dedicated to improving
leadership and communication, especially in the areas
of business, healthcare, and education.

Our mission is to inspire and empower our readers and
seminar participants to achieve success through value-
based, conscious leadership and generative collaboration.